The Lady and The Legacy

Take a Bow Enid Collet

PATRICIA KEEGAN

DEDICATION

This book is dedicated to one of my best teachers Enid Collett. What I have learned from her sincerity, kindness, and dedication has helped me in my journey so far.
I had great respect for Enid and her regard for humanity.

FOREWORD

There are thousands of extraordinary people in history, who have accomplished such great feats , it has changed the world. Yet no one knows who they really are.

One such great lady was the eponymous Enid Marjory Collett of Shoreham's state of art Lifeboat, the Enid Collett.

When I realized that no one seemed to have a hint of this captivating individual's personality, I felt it was my duty to enlighten them, especially the Shoreham lifeguard Station, where she has saved so many lives.

The characters of many famous people are lost forever once they have passed away. It seems a great pity that so many gifted personalities whose name goes down in history are soon forgotten, other than, of course, what they were famous for.

Very often, we are left to the devices of our own imagination. However, when this happens, we can sometimes draw a blank or, worse still, make incorrect assumptions.

I have often wondered about famous people myself. What were they really like, their quirks, their daily habits? How did they look? What was their true personality?

Were they friendly, social people, or were they loners?

So, rather than letting you imagine something that may be totally untrue, I have filled in the spaces for you.

I want to share with you Enid Collett's fascinating life story. To include all about what led up to the decision she made to fund the Shoreham Tamar lifeboat having no connection with the sea or anything to do with it.

After all, she came from a long line of farmers.

Almost all of her estate was left to the RNLI at Shoreham by Sea, and a smaller donation was made to the National Trust and other worthy charities.

The eponymic Enid Collett was born at the turn of the century. She was a farmer's daughter who lived in a Cambridgeshire village. Most of her life was spent working in the theatre world.

That is what you will be told about her when you take the tour of the magnificent state of art Shoreham Tamar Lifeboat, the Enid Collett, for they know nothing else.

As Claire Saunders Wicks said recently to me, it is a shame that so very little is known about the lady whose decision it was to make a difference to Shoreham by Sea Coastal front.

When Claire took the tour of the Enid Collett and asked for more information about Enid, she was told that was all they knew.

Claire decided to do a study of her own, but although she researched extensively, she was disappointed to find no more information.

I can understand this, as although Enid was an exceptionally gifted theatre manager and director, she was shy and modest. She would have despised being brought into the limelight and chose to disappear into the background when it came to praising. However, nothing pleased her more than to see the success of the thespians and the theatre alike.

The pleasure she derived from helping when and where she could, with everything that was asked of her, and giving 110 percent at all times, was enough for her.

I had a dream in May 2021. It was about Enid. She was encouraging me to get on with her story.

I absentmindedly drew a picture of what I had seen in my vision. Then, I wrote the words "May Day, May Day, Answering the Call," on it.

When I had finished, I made a mental note to get on with Enid's story.

A few days after, I was shocked to see that the RNLI was making a National appeal for donations. The slogan was:-

"May Day, May Day, Will you answer the Call?"

A shiver ran down my spine when I saw it.

Even as I write, I still shiver as I think of it. I am sure Enid was giving me the shakeup that I needed.

I decided there and then to put together my notes made in 1996, along with my memories and research, to reveal the mystery of her story.

So without further ado, I present to you her fascinating story.

CONTENTS

CHAPTER ONE

In the heart of Abbots Ripton, Huntingdon, on a thriving mixed farm in the middle of winter, just seven months after the end of the second Boer war, a baby girl was born to Alice Maud and William Collett.

Her name was Enid Marjory Collett.

It was Thursday, 6th of November 1902, and she was William and Alice's second child, born at Brooklands Farm, Abbots Ripton Huntingdonshire, about 4 miles north of Huntingdon. The same farmhouse that her sister Ruby had been born in, in 1900. The cottage was on the land of Lord De Ramsey.

William Collett had also been born on Lord De Ramsey's ancient acres.

Abbots Ripton is a primeval settlement. It is mentioned in the Domesday Book, written as Riptune. It is also said to have derived from the Anglo-Saxon word Riptune meaning wood or woodland. There is an abundance of woodland in the parish.

The 18th-century Abbots Ripton Hall stands on the grounds of the old manor that was there in 1086. It appears that even at that early time, there was a church and a priest on the land.

Abbots Ripton is reputed to have gotten its name from the old English vernacular, Rip, meaning strips of land, and Tun, meaning farm or homestead. Abbots Ripton Hall was a monastery where monks established arable land and fisheries.

So, it followed that Enid was born to a successful line of farmers in a settlement that was adept in agriculture.

Abbots Ripton had had its share of disasters. It was notable for the Railway disaster on 21st January 1876, when the Flying Scotsman was destroyed during a terrible snowstorm, causing havoc in its wake.

Even though William Collett had strong ties to Abbots Ripton, in 1908, he bought the house at 78 High Street Great Shelford Cambridgeshire and moved his young family there.

As I learned from Parish Council records, he didn't cut the ties immediately, and much of his work was still carried out there. In fact, I recall Enid telling me one day that while she was at boarding School in Huntingdon, in her teens, how embarrassed she was when she and her school friends had encountered her father while leading a cow right past the playground at her school. I am sure he didn't walk the animal from Great Shelford.

It was not long after the death of Queen Victoria in 1901. No wonder it was an exciting time to be born into an era such as that. It was a new age. All that had gone before seemed to have died with the old Queen

It appeared that the nation had grieved with Victoria for her beloved Albert.

The old Queen had set the trend with her long black clothes and subdued ways, and it had rubbed off onto England for many years, but anything was possible in this new modern age.

Black mourning clothes started to vanish, and the bustle on ladies' gowns had completely disappeared from fashion by 1906, along with the prudish dress implemented by Queen Victoria and the strict idea that women belonged at home in the kitchen.

The 20th century brought hope, excitement, wild ideas, and inventions into modern England. The colorful coquettish Edward Seventh, Queen Victoria's beloved Bertie, now reigned, and a new way of life began to emerge for the whole of England.

The foundations were made in the early years for the poor, for what later became known as the Welfare State.

The class distinction, however, was still rife. But things were gradually changing.

The Education Act, or Balfour Act as it was also known, was passed in 1902 and set the pattern for basic and secondary education.

A rapid awareness of global warming was now taking place, even though not yet fully explored or understood.

The world was changing rapidly. Never before in the history of England, it seemed, had the world and its understanding of it become as apparent as it had at the turn of the century.

H.G. Wells' novels about time travel and space were becoming more realistic by the day, with Jules Verne's (novelist and poet of the time) publication of Space exploration in 1903 showing that it was, indeed, theoretically possible.

It was a modern society, one of the most electrifying times known in history, and a camaraderie never known before.

My story begins in the summer of 1994. As my old car rattled up the unmade and, rather, the driveway of The Laurels 78 High Street, I saw two elderly figures hastily walking down the path towards me.

I was surprised to learn that the taller sprightly lady was Enid Collett, the 95-year-old lady I had come to care for. The smaller person was her friend and companion, Wendy. I learned later that Wendy was the daughter of Enid's late close friend. She had come to stay with her until help, me, had arrived.

I had been told to make my way to Enid's mid-morning. I got there in good time, just before ten a.m.

I abruptly stopped my old car, got out, and introduced myself.

"How nice to meet you. We are just going to the co-op to get some lunch. Do you like soup?" asked Enid.

Well, that was a pleasant surprise. Of course, you never know how people are going to react to your arrival. But one thing I have learned throughout the course of my life is that it's your own attitude that counts. So, I always have an open mind, never expect a particular outcome, and just wait and see.

At that time, I didn't realise, as I watched the pair running down to the shop that I would be embarking on one of the most fascinating journeys in my life so far.

When Larry, the manager of my care agency, had told me that my mission was to tend to the needs of a frail old lady, ninety-five years old, who had recently suffered a stroke, I expected to see her sitting, waiting for me to arrive, not running down the driveway to meet me.

"Well, yes, that would be lovely,"

I told her and drove up and waited outside the house, where she had told me to park my car.

I sank back in my seat, beginning to feel relaxed already.

I had travelled forty miles from my hometown to the unfamiliar Cambridgeshire village of Great Shelford. There in the midst of this busy, thriving village, set in the peaceful surroundings of a very large country garden full of vegetables, flowers, and trees, was the impressive home of this very special lady. It was my privilege to have come to care for her.

I took in my surroundings while waiting for them to come back.

Yes, I thought, I am going to like it here. How right I was. I stayed for two years on a week-on and week-off basis.

"The Laurels," 78 High St. Great Shelford, was right next door to the Co-Op, and Enid always bought her groceries there. She told me on many occasions how important it was to support local businesses.

As a live-in carer, I never knew what I would be walking into and could immediately sense what my stay would be like.

As promised, they were back in a jiffy. Wendy made me a cup of tea while Enid and I became acquainted.

Afterward, Enid told me lunch was expected at 1 pm and left me in the capable quiet hands of Wendy, who showed me around and then to my bedroom.

I unpacked my clothes and placed the photo of my sister Sandra and my dad, who were now together in heaven, on the small Victorian mantelpiece opposite the bed.

I laid myself down on the comfortable single bed and took in my surroundings. A marble Victorian washstand in the corner of the room held a small blue and white China jug and wash bowl.

The white cotton counterpane underneath me was old but pristine. I dreamily glanced through the small window overlooking the garden. I had a beautiful view and watched the trees swaying in the breeze. I smiled contentedly, breathing in the purity of the peaceful surroundings. The birds sang sweetly, and I closed my eyes for a few moments.

I must have dozed off and woken up suddenly. I went back downstairs quickly and was pleased to find that Enid was sitting in the lounge reading the newspaper.

I got on with preparing our lunch. It was just tinned soup, bread, butter, and cheese. It was ready and on the table in no time.

I found three embroidered napkins in the sideboard drawer, each in their separate napkin holders. Two carved wooden ones, and a little silver on, with her napkin folded in it.

Enid had informed me earlier that that was hers. I could have guessed as it had the initial E in one corner. Ruby's and Margo's napkin rings were lying beside it still, even though her two sisters had long passed away.

They had had the napkin rings since childhood, Enid had told me. I later learned that they had embroidered their own napkins as part of their curriculum at school. Being able to sew proficiently was considered essential for young ladies of such standing.

I picked up the beautiful bone-handled cutlery, admiring the fine craftsmanship as I did so, and set them on the farmhouse table with the beautiful old white linen cloth on it.

I went into the lounge to tell Enid that her lunch was ready. Wendy had gone home by now, and a smiling Enid followed me into the dining room.

Our lunch of tinned soup I had already poured into the bowls. Bread and cheese bought from the delicatessen counter in the butcher were on the antique plate in the centre of the table—a glass of water at each placement.

We spent an enjoyable lunch exchanging pleasantries, and afterward, Enid retired to her lounge and was not to be disturbed until tea time at 4 pm.

I began to wash up and clear away the things.

Looking around, I could see nothing had changed much here for the past 100 years.

The farmhouse had a nice homely feel to it. Mostly the furniture was Edwardian, all well cared for, and all of the good quality. The strong farmhouse pine table and chairs were probably 1900s, heavy, and very substantial.

It wasn't hard to imagine that I was back in the time when William Collett had first bought the farmhouse in the early 1900s and started farming here.

A door led off from the dining room out into the garden. The barn, now used as a log store, was immediately in front of it. I found my work straightforward, and Enid was undemanding. She had suffered a stroke and was recently out of the hospital, and although she never complained of illness, I kept a watchful eye on her.

It allowed me time to get my creative juices flowing, and what better place to do it than in Enid's home?

I had time on my hands, and I had stood on many a pleasant occasion at the door, listening to the tuneful voice of the blackbird. He always nestled on the gabled end of the roof while he sang. So this was my queue to find him some crumbs.

Enid always said she liked my poems and asked me to read them to her on many occasions whilst having breakfast. She was an encouraging listener and enthusiastically always wanted to hear what I had created next. She amused me by saying I was a poet laureate.

After our first lunch together, I finished tidying up and started my walk down the long driveway out onto the High Street. I looked up and down the road, then decided my first walk should be to explore the village.

Enid had said,

"It's important to support the local shops to keep them open. In fact, it hasn't changed at all much since I was a child,"

"Lloyds and Robinsons, the tailor's shop, was where the mobility shop is now, I recall, next to the Co-Op. The butchers are still in the same place opposite. The garage on the corner has been there as far back as I can remember. Our family has always used the local amenities."

A quaint village, some houses were the popular Suffolk pink, and one house had been painted blue. Enid had had her own opinions about this one. It seemed, later, when I spoke of it while telling her of my walk. It's an odd colour and didn't fit in with the rest of the old houses on the street.

St. Marys the Virgin Great Shelford

I walked along the High Street until I came to the ancient church of St. Mary the Virgin. Built in 1387, it was a magnificent find. I spent some time looking around this splendid building. I walked outside and read a few of the epitaphs on the graves. I found a nice bench to sit on and soak up the atmosphere, making a mental note to bring a pencil and my sketchpad on my next visit.

It was a pleasant day, but I felt unusually relaxed and contented, given my circumstances when I had left home and the difficulties I was experiencing at that time.

The stresses and strains of life, and the start of a new job, had led me, it seemed, to where I needed to be.

I slept well that night, in comfort and peace, and was up early the next morning, rested and ready to serve the needs of Miss Collett.

Breakfast in bed started the day for Enid at 9 am. She had a habitual meal of a pot of coffee, a medium soft-boiled egg, and a slice of toast.

Then, I didn't see her until she came downstairs after her ablutions at about

10 am.

Enid then, seated at the head of the farmhouse table, set about her routine business of answering any letters she had received.

She would then don her thin coat and wander around the garden, looking for a few fresh flowers to refill her vase.

She took everything in as she meandered around the neat sections of the garden.

A grass pathway led to where the usual type of vegetables grew, beans in neat rows, then potatoes, carrots, onions, and turnips.

There were a few of the more exotic plants too, which I experimented with by adding to the soups.

Then continuing along the same grass verge, a beautiful flower garden was to be found nestling at the back of the conservatory, at the rear of the house.

Enid spent many happy hours here resting in the garden room.

The bird table, thoughtfully placed among the flowers, provided entertainment from many different species of birds, bees, and, much to her amusement, the antics of the wily squirrel.

I can imagine that ruby being a keen horticulturist, learned a lot from the garden that was probably designed by farmer William Collett when he first moved there in 1908.

It had certainly been considered by someone with a lot of knowledge about planning and how nature works in the growing of certain plants alongside each other, to combat disease. Everything had been impressively and carefully thought out.

When she returned from the garden, she would tend to the cut flowers, snipping the bottoms off of them and returning them to the vase, throwing any away that were dying, then filling the vase with fresh water.

There was something calming about the way in which Enid went about her duties. She was well disciplined and knew what she was doing each morning, yet she was always ready to change anything at a moment's notice where necessary.

The next day, I wandered around the garden looking for new vegetables for our soup and experimenting with vegetables I hadn't used before. Our soups were always met with Enid's grateful approval.

Enid was a creature of habit, so it was soup again for lunch, with half a slice of bread and a small piece of Caerphilly cheese to follow.

I thought this would be a good time to bring up the question of what kind of food Enid liked to eat so that I could prepare menus.

While we were eating, and after enquiring if my soup creation was agreeable, I brought up the subject of her taste.

She stopped eating, placed her hands neatly in her lap, and looked straight at me.

"I eat anything but a rabbit!"

She stared at me wide-eyed. I waited to see what was coming next after her statement.

"When I was a child, nanny Polkington got us all ready early after breakfast one morning. Nanny Polkington, said Enid as if answering my unspoken question, was with me for the whole of my childhood. She stayed with us until she was quite old, and then she eventually moved into a nursing home.

Anyhow, as I was saying, nanny Polkington donned us in wellingtons, hats, and outdoor coats and told us,

"You are going out in the field to help your father."

We were all very excited about this rare outing with father.

Ruby, Stanley, and I were given little sticks each and went skipping off behind him down to the field in Great Shelford.

It was harvest time. The sun was shining, and I watched as the men were ploughing up the fields. It was all very pleasant.

As they did so, they exposed hundreds of little rabbit families.

I remember thinking how beautiful the little creatures were and how lucky we were to have this wonderful unexpected day out with father.

But suddenly, everything changed. It all happened so quickly that I couldn't quite understand it.

Then, Ruby grabbed my hand and nearly swept me off my feet. She dragged me down the field with her, almost lifting me off the ground.

Come on, she shouted excitedly.

She let go of my hand and went running off.

I just stood there and watched, horrified, as Ruby and Stanley chased the rabbits down the field.

Ruby was very good at it. She ran along as fast as she could, the poor little things ran very fast indeed, but they couldn't keep it up and just gave in, transfixed in terror while they were bludgeoned to death.

I realised then that I was supposed to do the same. I cried, kicked, and screamed as Ruby tried pulling me along with her again, wildly waving her stick about. Stanley was running to and fro as if it was a game.

This went on until the whole field had been ploughed up.

Ruby and Stanley, chasing and beating the heads of the poor defenceless little creatures, and grabbing them up while they were still crying, and me pleading with them to stop. It was awful!

Father scorned and made an awful fuss, and I was made to pick them up and walk home with the rest of my siblings.

"But they are not dead."

I wailed as the little rabbits writhed about in my hands. It was ghastly, and I just couldn't bring myself to do it.

I was not much of a farmer's girl. I'm afraid I must have been a great disappointment to my father.

But, of course, that was farming. We had to live. He sold the rabbits to the butcher across the road in Great Shelford.

However, I remember that every time I walked past the butchers, I saw them hanging up in the window, and I winced.

From that day on, it was a regular occurrence when we went shooting with father, I was forced to carry the writhing creatures after they had been shot. I suppose he thought it would make me stronger. But I never got over it."

Then straightening up her shoulders again, she looked me in the eye and said. "So, I don't eat rabbit!"

Enid had told the story with such vividness that it wasn't hard to see it clearly in my mind's eye.

I soon got to realise that Enid had hundreds of little stories like that to tell me. Naturally, I was fascinated, and over the months and years I stayed with her, I learned more about her personality and the sort of life she had led.

Every day brought with it a new interesting story. I began to look forward more and more to my entertaining lunch with Enid.

For instance, she told me the following day about how corn used to be sold in her younger days.

"Things have changed dramatically in the course of my lifetime."

She began.

She took a sip of her soup and nodded to me approvingly.

I'd made a particularly nice one that day with vegetables and herbs from the kitchen garden. She finished her bread and cheese, laid her hands in her lap, and continued her tale.

"Where was I?

Oh yes, things are so different nowadays. For example, how do they sell corn nowadays?"

I was quick to realise that I was about to have another history lesson.

"How did your father sell his corn, Enid?"

I encouraged.

Responding, as I knew she would, she stared thoughtfully ahead of her as if reminiscing, hands folded neatly in her lap.

"Well, I remember my father going to the Corn exchange on a Saturday, taking with him a few samples of ears of corn. These he would show to anyone who was interested in buying them."

She stopped briefly as if reliving the memory.

"Then, they would take them in the palm of their hand like this,"

She demonstrated by rubbing and rolling her hands together (obviously how she had seen it done as a child in the early 1900s)

"To see what the quality of the corn was like. Then, if they were satisfied with it, they would order how many hundredweight they wanted. So simple!"

She said, holding up her hands to empathise with the fact.

"Now, Corn Exchanges are used for dances, jumble sales, and goodness knows what else. I don't know anything about anything anymore,"

She finished wistfully.

And yet, when I made her bed this morning, I noticed that she was halfway through reading an 800-page book, The Political Life of John Major. Hardly a book for the faint-hearted and someone who knows nothing.

Stories like this, about Enid's childhood, I had found particularly interesting.

She had led a privileged life in the middle classes, and although there was a lot of poverty all around her, as a child, she had been oblivious to it. So it must have been quite enlightening, to say the least, when she ventured out into the big wide world.

When Enid spoke to me of her childhood, it was clear that there could be no contact with the common poor.

"We were not allowed to play with the village children.

They had NITS!"

She exclaimed, feigning a look of horror. Although I couldn't help smiling at the way she said this, with a look of affected shock, it was very much a way of how things truly were.

In the early 1900s, while Enid was growing up in the lap of luxury, there were many hungry and shoeless children on the streets. Children, as young as the age of ten years, trying to scrape a living doing odd jobs or whatever work they could find, just so they could eat. They did anything they could, such as chimney sweeping, being pit boys and girls, working on the farms, and being servants, which was common practice at this time.

Tragic accidents of all kinds resulted from child labour and abuse, and many lives were lost.

Accidents of all kinds have been reported.

In the newspaper archives, I found this report of an accident in Great Shelford when Enid was about 14 years old.

Wagon Accident: - A serious accident occurred to George Benstead, a Great Shelford lad of six years. He was walking beside a wagon in Mr. Wright's field and stumbled and fell, the wheel passing over his arm, breaking it in three places. He also hurt his ankle, the shoe being torn off his foot. Dr Magoris was called in and sent the boy to Addenbrookes Hospital, where he was progressing slowly.

This account of a child work-related accident was by no means an exception. Although it didn't say, he was probably a farmer's boy, either working on his own or with his parents.

After the death of Queen Victoria, many changes were taking place, especially in middle-class society. Housewives, with not much better to do other than embroidery or reading, now took the chance to become women in their own right. Some of them were very strong. Alice Collett, Enid's mother, was no exception. To help the poor, she had collected subscriptions from her friends and the villagers in Great Shelford. Enid still had her accounts, and she showed them to me one afternoon while we were having tea.

It was a rare treat for me to join her for this, and it was especially for the purpose of showing me her mother's things, along with old photographs.

I particularly remember the photo of Enid with her father. Ruby and Stanley were standing beside him after a day's shooting, and he proudly showed off some of the rabbits he had caught that day. Some were tied to a stick that he had over his shoulder, and Ruby and Stanley held one in each hand by the rabbits' legs.

Enid had also stood next to them, but it was evident by the look on her face that she was downcast.

Another photograph showed Enid as a young girl, about 15, punting in the river with a school friend in St. Ives Huntingdon. One on the steps at school in her tennis outfit, with a friend, after a game of tennis. Enid had enjoyed playing tennis for much of her life.

It is such a great pity that I have been unable to trace the whereabouts of the abundance of photographs that she showed me.

However, it was a grim reminder of the difference between the classes, as the majority of girls of that age were working hard for a living.

Class distinction still prevailed in the early 20th century, and it would have been frowned upon for Enid, a middle-class child, to have had such contact with the poor. Nevertheless, her mother was a thoughtful, considerate person and was trying to make a change in her own way, along with many other middle-class housewives. It was justifiably a time of change in the post-Victorian age.

I am sure that she made a difference to at least some of the poor and deprived children of Cambridge.

There were wealthy, caring people like Alice Maud Collett all over England trying to change the world for the better.

In May 1913, it was reported that Suffragettes had tried to blow up the Railway Crossing in Grahams Lane.

They had used a treacle tin with a bootlace inside, connected to a small firework, surrounded by cotton wool. It was soaked in oil and lumps of charcoal. On the outside were scrawled Votes for Women.

Enid's father sounded as if he had strong opinions of his own.

He had been a parish councilorcouncillor for Upwood and Ravely.

He was used to making decisions and organising much of what happened in and around the villages.

One account, in 1905, shown here, was when some people had fallen behind with the rent on their allotments. He had proposed that they be given two weeks to amend payments. If the money was not then forthcoming, the land should be given up.

Accounts.
Proposed by Mr. William Collett,

Seconded by Mr. Reginald J. Kidman, and resolved that the undermentioned accounts be passed and that cheques be drawn for same,

viz.:- £ s d SerjeantSergeant & Son re 'Jubilee Well.' 1 1 0 Gilding, Henry Pump repairs. 8 9 Honeybun, E. W. Election expenses. 8 10 Papworth, Charles Gravel. 1 4 0 Kennell, George Carting Gravel. 1 12 0 Margetts, C. B. Quit rent to Lady Day '05 6 11 £5 1 6

Allotment Arrears, Payment to be pressed. The Clerk reported the undermentioned Allotment holders still in arrear with rent due last Michaelmas, viz.: - Bedford, George 2/8/2, Shelton, Joseph 6/2 and Shelton Sr. Edward 6/2 when it was proposed by Mr. William Collett, seconded by Mr. George Thompson, and resolved that the Clerk write to them, giving fourteen days' notice for payment thereof, failing which, the Council will be obliged to provide them with notice to quit and give up possession of their respective Allotments.

Many people relied on the allotment to supplement their meagermeagre wages and keep the rest of the villagers in food. There was a lot of bartering going on in those days. It must have been devastating to have had to give up their livelihood, but of course, there had to be laws, and they had to be upheld. Tenancy agreements were drawn up by the landowners.

A Tenancy Agreement dating back to 1846 serving the Parish of Husbands Bosworth in Leicestershire states:

"Every occupier is expected to attend divine service on Sundays, and any occupier who digs potatoes or otherwise works on their land on Sunday shall immediately forfeit the same."

Although William Collett went along with government laws, he had strong opinions of his own, too, of what he deemed was necessary and what wasn't.

Enid told me one day over lunch that she remembered how in 1908, moving the clocks backward and forwards was discussed in the English government. After that, a lot of people in England began to do this, but it wasn't made law until as late as 1966.

"Father was adamant that we did not change the clocks. Greenwich, meantime, had been adopted in 1888, and it was this that he adhered to, seeing no benefit from changing.

Consequently, we never knew what the time was, she told me, because some people changed the clocks back and forth, and some didn't."

Enid gravely told me, while she was at St. Ives school for young ladies, that in 1918, Spanish "Flu had found its way into society, and was responsible for at least 500 million deaths all over the world."

It was caused by the H1N1 virus, with genes of avian origin, and was identified in the spring of 1918 in the United States of America in military personnel.

It spread rapidly all over the world, and having no vaccines or antibiotics to treat the virus, all that could be done was to isolate people, step up hygiene and limit public gatherings.

People walked the streets only when absolutely necessary, masked for protection, much like they do today with the recent pandemic (speaking in 2021.) They were as terrified then as people are now of Covid.

Many were fearful of leaving their homes. No one knew if they were to be wiped out as a nation. But like all diseases, it eventually passed, and the country began to breathe easily again, leaving the devastating destruction in its wake.

CHAPTER TWO

"Father was born at Brooklands farm, Abbots Ripton, on Lord De Ramsey's land."

Enid stopped eating and rested her hands gently in her lap, as she was apt to do when beginning a story.

I had artfully prompted her, prior to this, for another anecdote while we were enjoying our lunch.

"His unmarried younger sister Emma, lived there until she became quite old and couldn't possibly manage by herself any longer."

In my research, I found that Mr. William Collet, Enid's father in the 1881 census, was seen to be the head, living in Abbotts Ripton Huntingdonshire. The census also transcribed that his unmarried sister, Emma, 35 years old, also lived at the farmhouse.

The transcription also said he had seven men and two boys working for him on his farm.

Robert Circus is described as an indoor farm servant. There was another domestic servant Rebecca Peacock aged 15.

"This was where I and my brothers and sisters were all born. The house was very similar to this one.

A picture of it is hanging above the door leading into the lounge."

I was surprised. I thought that was a picture of 78 High Street. The Laurels. It looked exactly the same.

They were very similar. The same architect designed them.

"I remember the house had six bedrooms. There were lots of farm buildings in a very neat square. You know, the sort of thing, pigs in one corner, cattle in another, horses in another, and the carts in the far corner."

Enid then told me that she had recently been back to the place where she had been born to see what it was like.

"I was horrified to see that it was now a very old run-down pig farm. All the once neat corners had been reduced to rubble. Not as I remember it all."

Enid drew her chin into her chest and stared at me with a disapproving look of disbelief.

It's always sad when you go back to a place from your childhood and find it's nothing like the fond memories you have stored in your mind.

It appears that William must have been a very good organizer and businessman. For not only was the farm run with proficiency, but as I was beginning to find out, he was an active member of the community as a parish councillor.

I feel his aptitude for this rubbed off onto Enid, knowing her as I did now.

Whilst researching recently, I came across this interesting information concerning Enid's father.

On December 4th, 1894, the Parish Council at Ravely's first meeting was held at the National School at 7 pm.

Records of the minutes of this meeting showed that Enid's father, Mr. William Collet was one of the thirteen to be handed in as electors. He was proposed for the office of District Councillor, along with one or two others, which had declined, so it was agreed to elect him.

The records of the minutes for the first meeting of this council were held on December 31st, 1894. Where it began with the documentation:-

Every notice of motion shall be in writing and be signed by a member of the council giving notice. It shall be given to the clerk of the council and shall be kept in his home or office, which book shall be open for inspection to every member of the council.

William Collet was a valuable member of the council from that day on until 1919, when it was proposed to stand again for the position with others. However, Mr Collett, this time, decided to decline the offer.

"Anyhow, now, where was I? Oh yes, my father was born on the farm owned by Lord De Ramsey of Abbotts Ripton. He was brought up on Brooklands farm. Hall farm? But we moved from there when I was about six.

My mother was a Grunwell. She was very well off, you know. She was twelve years younger than my father and came from Sawtry. Anyhow, when they married, my father continued farming in Abbots Ripton, but there were family arguments, and it was decided that my father buy the farm here in Great Shelford. I was about six when we moved.

CHAPTER THREE

"We moved to Great Shelford when I was six years old. There were fields all around us then, which father used for growing beans, turnips, oats, wheat, and corn crops.

It had been suggested in Parliament that some farmers should start to grow flax and tobacco, as this was more profitable than grain.

However, I don't remember my father growing tobacco; I think he stuck to more traditional methods.

Every year since medieval times, Shelford has held its annual Shelford Feast on the Recreation ground. It was and still is, always held on the 2nd week in July. In Enid's time, this would have been held in the Sports ground where Leeway Avenue is now. However, it was moved to the land behind The De Freville Arms in the 1930s. It was a grand affair in those days, with a fun fair provided by Stanley Thurston amusements. The last Shelford Feast was held there right up until the Second World War

After over fifty years, I am sure that everyone was delighted when it returned in 1994 as a way of raising money for the Shelford Primary School, which was suffering greatly from government cuts at the time.

Now, the Shelford Feast is still held today, and it raises much-needed funds for Shelford's young people and it also helps good local causes.

At the turn of the century, there were ploughing matches in the village

This was a great way for farmers' workman to show off their skills and great fun for everyone. This drawing of a ploughing match, held in Great Shelford, was found online. It was probably sketched at the Shelford Feast early on in the 1900s.

PLOUGHING MATCH SKETCHED FROM THE GREAT SHELFORD ROAD.

Enid always took an interest in village events and was supportive of local businesses. Although she told me that the village hadn't changed much at all, even after living and working away from home for years, she was surprised to see still the garage and many of the local shops still thriving on her return.

I loved walking and finding new routes. When I lived with Enid, I always found it enjoyable. She knew all the public footpaths and advised me on many occasions where to ramble when I was wondering where to go next.

I had already walked all around Great Shelford village and across the short bridge to Little Shelford.

Enid was amused to think that as you approached the bridge, you were in Great Shelford, then when you had crossed it, you were in Little Shelford.

"It's only a few steps."

She had laughed.

Her face changed, though, as she sadly remembered the great tragedy that had happened in the land adjacent to it.

"The Hall there had burned to the ground because the river cut off the fire engines. It was terrible."

I thought of Enid's words as I glanced over the bridge while out for my walk. There were tall trees and shrubbery now in place of the Little Shelford Hall. I thought then how devastating it must have been and such a great loss to the preservation society.

I found the newspaper cutting that was in The Cambridge Chronicle at the time of the tragic fire.

March 1907. Exciting scenes were witnessed at Shelford, where two cottages close to the railway station were gutted. The discovery synchronized with the passing of the GER express, and it's thought a spark from the engine alighted upon the thatched roof. In the absence of any fire appliance, helpers concentrated on removing the furniture, and every article, with the exception of the iron bedsteads, was carried to a place of safety.

I had to include this humorous snippet of information I found whilst researching events in Great Shelford about Mrs Plumb, the fruiterer. She sounds like a character from a children's storybook.

Apologies if I sound rude. All said in jest. She sounds like she was a wonderful, hardworking asset to the community.

Enid always said that trying to find a little humour in everything you do helps carry you along with the stresses and strains of life.

July 1937, the B.S.A. Company's offer of a brand-new bicycle to Britain's oldest woman cyclist brought several responses. Mrs Chedworth of Mortimer Street is sixty-three; she has been riding a bicycle since she was ten and has toured Ireland, Scotland, and much of England on it.

There are articles like this that really give you a feel of how times have changed over the years. Some say its progress, while others say it was not so stressful then. Enid always told me that trying to find a little humour in everything you do helps carry you along with the stresses and strains of life.

I have always tried to do this and have always enjoyed walking in nature.

16

Major roads can take minutes in a car to a place where it would have perhaps taken hours on a cycle. Only well-off people could afford cars in those days.

Luckily, Great Shelford and the surrounding villages are still very lush in parts, but if you are driving, you dare not take your eyes off the grey road, to admire it. This is where a leisurely ride on a bicycle is appreciated most.

When I used to be on my walks, it was hard to believe in 1994, that this well-built-up village, with the bustling high street and a bank next door to the Compass pub, at the end of the street where Enid lived, could once have been all greenery.

When I had exhausted the walks close to her home, Enid suggested I take a five-minute drive further down the road to Wandlebury, which was a particular favourite place of hers.

I later found out why when she began telling me stories of the years she spent in the theatre world, and the connection to it had to her very first employer.

I was amazed when I drove down station road and came to the Gog Magog Hills and
Wandlbury on the A1307. It was a vast and beautiful ancient land.

I explored as much of the area as I had time for and vowed to go back when I could to explore the rest.

When I got back, I made Enid's afternoon tea and settled myself in the library to jot down everything before I forgot.

Note 1. In Big letters.

I MUST BRING A LARGER NOTEPAD!

CHAPTER FOUR

One morning, soon after I had started caring for Enid, there was a tinkle on the ancient wall-mounted doorbell, reminiscent of a traditional shop bell.

Enid was busily cutting the stems off the bottoms of the flowers, on an old newspaper, on the farmhouse table in the dining room while I was clearing away breakfast things.

I dried my hands quickly on my apron and answered the door.

I was a little surprised to see an elderly, reddened-faced woman, breathless with her long walk up the driveway, leaning up against the wall.

She was dressed in an odd array of brightly coloured clothes.

She wore stripy multi-coloured stretchy leggings and a colourful paisley scarf around her neck, topped off by a woollen hat pulled snuggly around her head.

I noticed her odd holey fingerless gloves as she propped herself breathlessly up against the porch way door. What a feast for my eyes as I wondered what on earth this delightful, unexpected visitor could possibly want so early on this morning.

Before I had a chance to enquire what she wanted, Enid suddenly appeared behind me and exclaimed.

"Betty! What on earth is the matter?"

Betty's small frame bustled behind Enid, following her into the lounge.

With much puffing and blowing, Betty was almost in tears as she explained her tale of woe. "The electric wheelchair is at the bottom of your driveway," She whined.

"What am I going to do?"

Enid prompted me to make Betty some tea.

The delightful, eccentric Betty was about five feet tall with unkempt grey hair. She was probably in her seventies. Pleasant looking enough when she smiled, but she had too many worries, so she was always full of grief. Mainly about her son, Simon.

She was always dressed in a variety of flashy clothes which she bought from the jumble sale, then threw them out when they were dirty, so she wasn't troubled by washing them.

She would come on various days, usually early in the morning, and would pour her troubled heart out about Simon to the kind-hearted Enid.

"What on earth will become of him?"

I can still hear her say it now. I really sympathised with Betty at these times, as only a mother can.

Betty would burden herself, and whine about him, virtually all the time.

"I worry that he will be forever homeless. He never sticks to anything. How I wish John were here."

Betty's husband and Simon's father had passed away ten years previously.

Forever worrying about her son, I heard her on many occasions.

"Why has he to go off to a foreign country to teach? Why not stay and finish his degree in England and teach here."

She continued.

But it seemed that Simon was a free spirit, and after his marriage had broken down, he was trying to find himself again, making it difficult for him to settle for anything permanent.

Betty had terrible difficulty walking after having unsuccessful operations on both knees. I knew that the more this generous-hearted lady worried, the more pain she felt. Probably Enid did too.

Enid thought that the electric wheelchair that she no longer used would be a great help to her friend.

Betty whizzed about on it all over the place but continued to let the battery run down on it, finding herself in a great struggle.

When I returned with the refreshment in one of Enid's pretty cups and saucers, I could hear Enid's soothing voice comforting the sensitive Betty.

"Try to remember to put it on charge. I will get Kevin from the mobility shop to collect it."

Enid bought the wheelchair after she had had the stroke. However, she found she didn't need it after all and had made a gift of it to Betty.

I offered to drive Betty home, and Enid was soon on the telephone with Kevin, arranging the collection of Betty Morrison's wheelchair. Kevin delivered the scooter for her later that day.

Betty was a very amiable lady, but I was not expecting to see the beautiful house that she lived in.

I turned my car into Granham's Lane in Betty's direction and continued over the level crossing.

To my left, there were acres of lush green fields where six beautiful horses were lazily grazing.

To my right were more fields that stretched for miles. Scattered under the trees, the sheep were snuffling their noses into the grass.

It was a beautiful relaxing scene, and I began to wonder where on earth we were going.

Suddenly, Betty broke into my thoughts.

"Turn in here,"

She said.

I drove into the grounds, and there in front of me was the vast house of Betty Morrison. Granham's Manor. I was flabbergasted as Betty fumbled in her shoulder bag for her keys.

I watched her as she walked round the back of the huge house and entered the back door.

I imagine that these had probably been servants' quarters over the years. It seemed strange to me to think of her going in the back way.

She then turned and gave me a wave and shut the door.

Granham's Manor, Betty Morrison's House, set on acres of land in Granham's Lane.

There seems to be more information on this house than on many others that I have researched.

The manor, later known as 'Valence,' 'Moyne's,' 'Grenden's,' or 'Granham's,' probably derived from the three hides held in 1086 by Peter de Valoyne's in chief.

A William le Moyne (Monachus) held land in Great Shelford in 1138; in 1198, another William le Moyne held 100 acres there, probably the former Valoyne's land.

There has been a manor here since the Anglo-Saxon period, with artefacts of such being found in the ditches adjacent to it.

Early morning visits were a regular occurrence for Betty. On a fairly ordinary Saturday morning in June, I remember Enid silently going about her business when suddenly, the stillness was broken, by the tinkle of the doorbell, sounding lazily throughout the house.

I made my way towards the door and could see Betty's worried features pressed up against the window pane.

All traces of fear disappeared from Betty's anxious face as I opened the door and greeted her with a warm smile. Enid is fine and will be with you very soon, I said, as I showed her into the lounge.

It was then that I noticed that Betty was looking very smart indeed. So I looked into her face.

"You look very nice today, Betty,"

I mouthed.

She beamed at me, then laughed dismissively with a wave of her hand.

"I am going to meet Prince Charles this afternoon. My son is playing polo with him at Windsor."

Betty and John Morrison had two sons, I learned, and a daughter. The daughter was very attractive and had won a beauty contest in her younger years.

Betty had announced the event, with no more ardour, than if she were planning a shopping spree!

I had come to know Betty quite well by now and found her very modest and interesting.

I was always learning something new from her. For instance. One lunchtime, while Enid and I were supping soup, I asked Enid about the picture of the plans of a warship I had seen on her kitchen wall.

"Oh, that is the Drawing of John Morrison's Greek Trireme."

There were so many drawings on her wall. Some are done by professional artists, some by amateurs. All signed. It mattered not to Enid whether they were famous or not. If she liked them, they would go on the wall. However, this sketch intrigued me.

I nodded, not really understanding but knowing that when Enid stopped eating and placed her hands gently in her lap, an interesting story was about to unfold and that all would be revealed soon enough.

Enid explained how she had met Betty 25 years previously when Enid was chairman of the local conservative party.

"I had retired from the theatre and had come home from London to take up residence again at the family house."

I think Enid probably took after her father in her ability and fervour for interest in her community.

"Margo had also retired and had come home to live. So together, we decided to buy Ruby out.

Ruby was settled in Cornwall at the time,"

Enid said by way of explanation.

"Anyhow, as I was saying,"

Enid closed her eyes for a few moments, recalling the facts.

"The position of chairman became available, and I was asked to take it on. As I had nothing better to do with my time, I said I would. We used to hold the conservative meeting at The Granham's where Betty and John Morrison lived."

I had some very interesting times while I was in this post. Enid's face was alert and proud, and she pulled herself up in her chair, straightening her back.

"One being the time I was asked to a conference, when William Haigh, then aged sixteen, gave his first public speech. It was clear, even at that age that he was going to go far. I think it must have been his ambition even then to become a prime minister or something like that,"

She said,

"Otherwise, he wouldn't have been interested in public speaking."

Becoming focused again, Enid continued with her story.

"Well, coming back to the picture on the wall, John Morrison was quite well known for the reconstruction of the Greek Trireme. The Greek Trireme was an ancient warship in the 4th and 7th centuries BC.

The drawing in the kitchen was the plans of its reconstruction."

Enid went into great detail about this, and as usual, after our lunch, I quickly scribbled down what I could remember before I forgot.

Rather than leave these facts about John Morrison to memory, I have checked my notes with those I found on the internet.

John Sinclair Morrison.

John Sinclair Morrison CBE FBA (June 15th 1913-October 25th, 2000), who wrote under the name of J.S. Morrison, was an English Classicist whose work led to the construction of an Athenian Trireme, an ancient oared warship.

Born in 1913, Morrison was a professor of Greek and head of the classics department at the University of Durham from 1945-1950. He was a tutor at Trinity College Cambridge from 1950-1960, then vice master of Churchill College from 1960-1965, when he became the first president of the University College, later named Wolfson College.

He was considered an expert on the Greek Trireme, the oared warship of the Athenian classical golden age. He is best known as one of the founders in 1982, with Charles Wiillink, another classics teacher, John Coates, a naval architect, and Frank Welsh, a banker, who came together to test his theories out by building a full-size reconstruction. In 1984 the Greek government promised funding, and in 1987 the Olympias was commissioned.

With W.T. Williams, Morrison wrote Greek Oared Ships| 900-322 BC. Long Ships and Round Ships (1980) with John Coates, The Athenian Trireme: The History and Reconstruction of an Ancient Greek Warship (1986) with J.F. Coates, Greek and Roman Oared Warships (1996), and other works.

His elder daughter, Annis Garfield, the classicist and author, was an alumna of Girton College and was voted the most beautiful girl in Cambridge in 1968.

In 1991 he was awarded the Caird Medal of The National Maritime Museum, jointly with John Coates.

In 1989 he was awarded an Honorary Degree (Doctor of Letters) by the University of Bath.

John Morrison died on October 25th at the age of 87, and Betty missed him terribly.

This is a photo of him aboard the reconstruction of the Greek Trireme.

We finished our soup, and after another very informative history lesson, I set about clearing away the lunch things.

During my two-hour break, I ventured out again to explore.

This time I had taken a ride on Enid's old bicycle, which she had lent me. I cycled to the end of the village, stopping for a while at the level crossing, admiring the immensity of the countryside and the manor house, and thought of Betty inside.

I cycled up the top of Granham's Lane, where I could see Addenbrookes Hospital in the distance. If I squinted slightly, it looked as if there was no busy road at the bottom of the hill. It continued for miles. The breath-taking view stretched right across Wandlebury and The Gog Magog Hills.

When I got back to the house, Enid had a visitor. A smart well-groomed lady from Little Shelford, whom Enid introduced as Mrs. Barbara Bacon. I couldn't help noticing that she was impeccably dressed in a well-cut suit. She was very well made up, and her hair was beautifully styled. I was intrigued to know who this cultured well-spoken lady was.

I made afternoon tea for them both and took mine into the library with me.

There, overlooking the greenery of the profuse trees in the garden, my inspiration was fuelled again.

My life at Enid's was becoming more fascinating by the day. I scribbled down a few quick notes before I forgot.

Little did I know who our special guest was at the time.

Barbara's father was an English Cricketer, Godfrey Keppel Papillon, 1867-1942. He was born in Lexdon Manor, Essex.

Barbara Papillon 1905-200, and Tom Bacon 1902-1992, had met through the church. They married in 1934 and moved to Little Shelford in 1946.

Dr Francis Thomas Bacon, Barbara's late husband, was born at Billericay in Essex in 1904. He studied engineering at Trinity College Cambridge.

Mr. Francis Thomas Bacon OBE was renowned for engineering the development of the first practical hydrogen-oxygen fuel cell.

In every Apollo flight, they had executed faultlessly.

After the successful lunar landing on July 11th, 69, Mr. and Mrs Bacon met Neil Armstrong, buzz Aldrin, and Michael Collins at a reception at 10 Downing Street.

A photograph, signed by the astronauts, of the first footstep on the moon was presented to him.

It is shown here.

President Nixon was reported to have said;

"Without you, Tom, we wouldn't have gotten to the moon."

Francis Thomas Bacon passed away on 24th may 1992, aged 98, leaving Barbara a widow.

Enid used to go to Mrs Bacon's house regularly, every month, to play Bridge with her and a couple of friends. Other times Barbara would come for afternoon tea. I always found her very pleasant.

Barbara respected Enid and would value her opinion. I remember conversations between Enid and Barbara that I had walked in on various occasions about whether Barbara Bacon should put her son's treasured paintings into a vault at the bank for safekeeping. She was afraid that she would have a burglary as they were very valuable. In my ignorance, I remember thinking that she was related to Frances Bacon, the artist, not the scientist responsible for the success of the landing on the moon.

The end of another week and my return home was to a very different life altogether. I couldn't wait to get back and see what other surprises were in store for me, as I knew there would be.

CHAPTER FIVE

I loved the feel of this place. I felt as if I was walking through a door into another world. It brought me some much-needed solace; in the difficult life, I had left behind.

The old farmhouse and its furniture seemed to have soaked up the energy of its inhabitants over the past hundred years or so. Yet, in the time that Enid had lived there, it seemed nothing much had changed, by way of furniture and soft furnishings, since she was a child.

It was more like visiting an old friend than going to work. There was always something new and interesting to learn.

I strolled around the garden, looking for herbs and vegetables for the table, and stopped and had a chat with the gardener.

Enid had three gardeners, I came to realize.

There was John, to whom I was talking. He came from Bury St. Edmunds and had been there for five years. He came to do the vegetable garden and any heavy work.

Then, there was a local couple of women gardeners who had been there for many more years.

I prepared a special meal of tasty vegetable soup with my produce from the garden and then went to fetch Enid for our lunch at 1 pm.

We sat down, and soon Enid was telling me all about her childhood and her nanny, whom she had known since she was a baby.

"I probably loved nanny Polkinton more than my mother.

Well, I knew her more, said Enid. So, I was bound to."

She said, as if by way of explanation.

"Nanny Polkington was the first person I saw on waking up in the morning and the last person to see before I went to sleep. She was a very kind, fair person, and she loved us children all the same.

Father was always out early in the mornings, working, so we didn't see much of him, and mother was constantly busy with her work as treasurer of the Conservative Party.

She also used to collect subscriptions from the villagers to help the poor. I still have her account books. I will show you one day."

Enid said, looking me in the eye.

"Mother had quite a few friends in the Conservative Party and was far too busy to tend to us children."

She laid her hands in her lap again before proceeding. I loved these little stories of Enid's. I was beginning to get quite a collection of them now.

"We only saw mother and father for about an hour a day. That was in the evening. After making sure we were clean and tidy and ready for bed, nanny Polkington would take us to mother and father. We used to then spend an hour with them playing hunt the thimble or a card game like happy families. You know, the sort of thing. After this, we kissed mother and father goodnight, and nanny Polkington would take us to bed.

"We had very few actual friends."

She said as an afterthought,

"We weren't allowed to play with the children in the village.

They had nits! She exclaimed with a look of feigned horror."

"Oh, that's a shame, Enid. How did you feel about that?"

"Well, I had my brother and sisters to play with. I suppose I would have noticed it more if I were an only child."

She said casually.

"My mother's cousins came sometimes. We were allowed to play with them."

On finishing her soup, as if remembering more to her story, she continued.

"We used to have primrose parties at Easter, and blackberry parties, and of course, for my birthday in November, we had firework parties."

She smiled.

"They were great fun,"

She continued.

"Mother used to collect the children in the buggy."

"Your cousins?"

"Well, she had quite a few friends in the conservative party, so their children sometimes came too."

I listened attentively.

"Now, what was I saying?"

"About your parties,"

I had prompted Enid.

"Oh yes, we had wonderful parties."

Her eyes were sparkling as she recalled her happy childhood.

"All the children would sit in the buggy, and we would collect blackberries or pick primrose. Then we would all have afternoon tea on the lawn. It was great fun! Then mother would take them all home again in the buggy."

Suddenly her face clouded over. I watched and became a little concerned.

"However, I remember one terrible day,"

She said.

"My brother, my sister, and I were all in the buggy with mother, and we were just passing over the level crossing by the station when suddenly, Jumbo the pony came to a sudden halt!"

Her eyes widened, and she sat bolt upright, holding me captivated.

"We could hear the train coming.

It was terrifying!

Mother tried desperately to get him to move, but he just stood there!"

Her face paled as she continued her story.

"My heart was beating so fast; I was afraid to breathe. I remember squeezing my eyes shut, just waiting for the impact. Then, seconds before it reached us, he reared up, almost tipping us all out, and then galloped off. I feel quite ill thinking about it."

"It must have been petrifying Enid,"

I said.

This started another story as we were finishing our bread and cheese.

"Nanny Polkington very often took us all to play in the fields together for a picnic. We loved it, and as we got older, we were left to enjoy the peace and quiet on our own while she was busy.

It was great fun. We used to play in the barns too, sometimes."

Even though we had come from totally different backgrounds, I could feel the joy as Enid replayed her memories.

I have fond recollections of playing in the old Oast Houses of Kent when going for hop-picking with my family, and I felt a warm glow as I listened.

Enid held me spellbound with her stories. She was a wonderful storyteller.

"But one ghastly day, Stanley climbed right to the top of an enormous haystack in the barn.

Suddenly he slipped and was hanging upside down by his foot!"

Ruby Margot and I stood in shocked horror for a moment before Ruby took control.

Quickly get some hay!"

"Margot and I sprang into action at Ruby's command.

We pulled out as much hay as we could from the great stacks. I suppose it wasn't much at all, really, with our small hands.

Ruby, swiftly tried to make a mattress on the floor beneath Stanley to land on.

Then she waved us back with her hand.

"Stay there!"

She shouted at us.

Then without further ado, she started to climb the great haystack.

Up, up, up she clambered until she was almost on top of the giant haystack.

I thought the whole lot was going to come crashing down, with Ruby and Stanley buried beneath it.

I remember squeezing Margo's little hand to reassure her, but I was so terribly frightened.

Just as Ruby was nearing the top of the hayloft, his foot slid out, and Stanley came tumbling to the ground!

I was horrified!"
She said, as her face darkened.
"I felt sure he would break his neck or something."
"Oh God," I said,
"What happened? Was he very hurt?"
Enid's eyes were bigger than I had ever seen them before,
"Not at all,"
She said in amazement.
"He just stood up and brushed himself down.
However, the shock of it all made me feel sick for the rest of the day."
I smiled warmly at her as I thought of the younger sensitive Enid.

I could see in my mind's eye that all those years ago, how poor Enid would have watched, worried to death, over the fate, of the unfortunate Stanley.

She had been terrified that he would have become the victim of a terrible accident.

While the formidable Ruby took charge of the whole situation, Stanley had come tumbling down like a performing acrobat in a circus. I was beginning to learn more about the Collett children and Enid's gentle nature more and more with every story.

It seemed to me that she had always been a genuinely caring person. This would have been too unbearable for her even to contemplate such a disaster.

These wonderful conversations always happened at meal times, sitting comfortably around the old-fashioned pine table and chairs that had been a part of the house for as long as Enid could remember.

Continuing the next day on the story of her childhood, I had asked her about schooling.

Enid responded at once.

"I was taught by a live-in governess. I remember she wore a blue uniform, similar to the one nanny Polkington wore. All the servants wore uniforms."

I hadn't thought about this. But, of course, it makes sense now. The lower classes had to know their place.

Many upper-middle-class children were brought up to think that the lower classes were inferior, dirty, and ignorant. By the way, Enid had talked about the village children having nits, I expected she was no exception to the rule.

"Now, where was I? Oh yes, then, I was sent to a small boarding school in Clacton by the Sea, run by my mother's sister. I hated it,"
Enid said, shaking her head.

"Luckily, I didn't have to go there for long, as soon after, war broke out."
It was the first time I had ever heard anyone say that!

Most people spoke about the terrible Second World War as shocking.

Before this, Britain was considered a prosperous, thriving country. The classes knew where they stood. After the war, the class distinction started to change.

Many men came home mentally and physically wounded, only to find that their homes had been bombed out of existence. They had lost wives, children's mothers, and fathers.

Although she would have suffered the consequences of war, Enid, however, being a middle-class protected child, would not have had to endure hunger and hardship as of others.

The 1914 war was global and lasted for four years, leaving devastation of destruction in its wake.

Then, with a smile, she added.

"Mother said we had to come home to the country, as we were too exposed right by the sea.

Ruby and I were sent to St. Ives Cambridgeshire boarding school. My mother had gone there when she was a child. I thoroughly enjoyed it there. I had lots of friends to play with, which was liberating as I had very few at home.

That's where we embroidered our table napkins, which you see in the sideboard drawer.

Schools in those days were quite different from what they are now. More often than not, young ladies of the middle classes were taught social grace and etiquette. Needlework and art were also part of their program."

I know that Enid particularly enjoyed tennis too.

It was not considered as important for girls to learn mathematics as it was for boys. This is because they were not being prepared for work so much as to how to manage a household and run a houseful of servants.

Since Queen Victoria had died and after the war, things were slowly beginning to change for the better.

However, middle-class young ladies were expected to get married to well-off gentlemen. So, to be attractive to men, demure and subservient, was mainly what was deemed to be most important in education.

Enid was not much interested in making herself pretty, wearing fashionable clothes, or in marriage. She loved the school, however, and sunk blissfully into the joys of punting, playing tennis, croquet, and other games, fitting for a gentleman's wife, blissfully unaware of what was expected of her in the future.

When she left school, however, she found she had not been prepared to earn a living. As she had said, there were only three choices available to her. So it must have come as quite a shock when she realized that her first choice was to get married to a nice gentleman. I am sure Enid must have had her share of admirers, but that wasn't what she wanted.

"I then had the choice,"

She said the word as if it had mocked her,

"To be a nurse, secretary, or a governess. I didn't much like the idea of any of them."

Her face had suddenly taken on a look of disgust.

More often than not, young ladies of the middle classes were taught social grace and etiquette, needlework art, and sports. I know that Enid particularly enjoyed tennis as she continued this game throughout her life.

Since educating girls of the middle classes, other than the ladily etiquettes, was not as essential as for boys, the girls knew not much about how they would earn a living if they did not marry a well-off gentleman.

However, after the 1914 war, things were slowly beginning to change for the better. A new kind of woman was emerging. Enid was no exception in wanting to be independent of men in general. Women wanted and knew how to get equality. This was a society that had been campaigning for years for the vote. Slogans were seen everywhere.

"Votes For Women."

Suffragettes tied themselves to railings, making small bombs to blow up railways. They did anything they thought might grab the attention of the male population and serve to promote women.

Meanwhile, Enid was continuing to be taught, very pleasantly, I might add, how to enjoy the finer things in life that might have been expected of her as a gentleman's wife.

How to satisfy a hardworking husband, art, craft, needlework classes, and other pastimes were all a young woman needed to know for life beyond school. Upper-middle-class ladies were not expected to go to work!

Enid left school at eighteen years old. Many working-class women in England had left school at the age of twelve or fourteen, some even younger. Many were, at this age, already married and bringing up families.

However, Enid's schooling had nothing to do with preparing her for work, in an ever-changing world, outside the shelter of her school for young ladies.

Nevertheless, middle-class young women were still expected to wed wealthy men. Therefore, it was mostly believed that education was most needed to be modest, obedient, and beautiful to men.

Enid was not interested in any of it at all. So she never tried to make herself look attractive to men, wear fashionable clothes, or get married in particular.

However, she told me she loved this school. She showed me photographs of her friend and herself punting on the River Cam, playing tennis, croquet, and other games. Being strong and healthy was also important. No self-respecting gentleman wanted a sickly wife.

For a spouse to be able to reproduce fine healthy children, especially sons, to carry on the family name was important.

However, by the time Enid had finished her schooling, times had changed. Enid didn't want that kind of life. Young women wanted more for themselves than just being someone's wife. Maybe a lot of young middle-class women didn't want to get married, but of course, that would then pose the question of how they were going to look after themselves financially and live in the way they were accustomed to.

So, when she left school, Enid found she had not been prepared to earn a living.

"I had to do something, though."

I listened attentively, interested to know why she was expected to go out to work. I thought that would be the last thing her middle-class mother would have wanted for her.

Was it her own choosing? Was she a little rebellious? Was it a stubborn way of making a stand? Or did she just not want to be a married woman?

Women were becoming more independent by the day. While the men were away fighting in the 1914 war, the women had become confident, brave heroes in their own right. But, for the most part, they energetically ran the country on their own in a way that made everyone sit up and take notice of the new-age women.

They didn't particularly want to give up that position now, and so the fairer sex continued to make themselves heard.

It was just one of the defiant ways to show the world that they deserved equality.

After years of being in the kitchen, pandering to the needs of a male population, women were now rebellious and beginning to show the world what they were really made of.

They had literally put on the trousers, drove tractors, ploughed fields, and daringly drove the underground trams.

They had worked dangerously in the munitions factories, soldiering on even when terrible fatal accidents had occurred. Undeterred, even when working on the explosive phosphorous, which turned the women's skin a yellow colour as they worked, earning them the name of the canaries.

"Britain would have come to a standstill if women hadn't gone out to work. They did every conceivable job there was to keep the country running as smoothly as it could during the dreadful years of devastation."

Enid said wistfully.

I wished I had asked Enid why Ruby's friends called her Colin and why Enid's, called her Peter.

In the 1920s, however, when women wanted equal rights with men, it was hardly surprising that some women wanted to adopt masculine names to go with their new standing.

I know Ruby was a very strong woman by how Enid spoke of her. I could imagine her striding about her business, in charge of every situation. While Enid was always willing to please her big sister and obeyed her every command when she was young.

"I suppose you could call her a tomboy, really. Ruby had a motorbike that she used to ride to work in Pampisford."

Enid was reminiscing again.

I knew Pampisford as a quiet little village on the outskirts of Cambridge, a few miles down the road from where Enid lived and close to Sawston.

"We were totally different characters; I just wanted a peaceful life most of the time."

"This was the age of the flappers. Wild music, shorts, skirts, short hair. Cigarettes in holders, strong drinks. Whatever the men did, the flappers did it too.

Of course, we all got disapproving looks from our elders," said Enid with a wry smile.

"But I was never a flapper, really. That kind of lifestyle and dress wasn't for me."

When Enid showed me a picture of herself in her twenties, with her new trendy haircut, however, I could see she wasn't entirely against the idea.

Along with scores of other young ladies of that era, Enid had her hair cut short. It was a defiant act that many were adopting at that time.

"I have smoked and drunk wine, talking with the men, until the early hours of the morning Enid told me with a twinkle in her eye.

That twinkle told me it was a far cry from what had been expected of her at the school for young ladies she had attended.

After all, in the upper classes, it had been accepted that men were apt to retire to the drawing-room, to smoke and drink strong liquor without any interference from women.

Since the war, fashion was changing along with everything else. As if women were promoting their newfound strength, trousers had become fashionable.

"Everyone, too, wore hats at that time. To be seen without a hat in the 1920s was unthinkable."

Enid was persistent, however, in resisting the invitation to find a nice young gentleman to marry. Times had changed over the years, and with the unfavourable idea of getting married, I suppose she had presented a problem to her family. So there was just one thing left to do. Get a job and support herself.

"The problem was there were very limited things I could do. I could become a nurse, a teacher, or a secretary.

Well, I wouldn't say I liked the idea of doing any of these things, but out of the three, I chose secretary. I then went off to Reading University to take a secretarial course.

Ruby was following in her father's footsteps, already doing gardening in the roundabout villages. She had a keen interest in Horticulture and was pursuing her career.

None of this interested Enid in the least, however. But at least Ruby hadn't succumbed to the marrying of a rich young gentleman. So, it gave Enid the encouragement that she needed.

"As I was nearing the end of my course. I was sent for an interview in Cambridge, close to where I lived.

I was very nervous at the thought of going out to work."

Enid had a new story to tell me every day, and with each new story, I was getting to know her more and more.

I was enjoying my work with Enid immensely.

Her tales were told with such clarification, even at the age of 95, and maybe a fading memory of mundane things, her mind was as sharp as ever. Yet, when it came to recalling past events, it seemed as if picking them out of a hat, one at a time.

Same place, different era. And yet, I could see it all!

"I rode on my bicycle the three miles to Cambridge. I had butterflies in my stomach as I stood looking up at the old building.

The Festival Theatre.

I wonder what it has in store for me, I thought."

CHAPTER SIX

With each story, I was transported, to a different world. I felt privileged, to be let into the clandestine, private, life, of Miss Enid Collett.

After lunch, when Enid retired to her lounge for an afternoon read of The Times, and maybe a little nap, in her chair, I would hurriedly tidy up so that I could jot down the notes while they were still fresh in my mind.

On my walks, I brought home uncommon sprigs of flowers and variegated leaves that I had found on my journeys through the overgrown footpaths. I painted their beauty back at the house in a state of bliss, in a world of dreams and days gone by.

I found I was always writing, sketching, or painting.

I drew inspiration from watercolours adorning the walls throughout the house and gifts from the botanic artist, a personal friend of Ruby, who worked at Kew Gardens.

Enid had told me when I asked about the paintings.

"They are accurate pictorial depictions of flowers, the emphasis being on science rather than just visual beauty. You see, a camera cannot capture the minute details that are necessary for scientific research."

I realized then that it was vitally important for these to be perfect for the expert horticulturalist Ruby.

The large number of autobiographies I found on the shelves, from talented film stars lining the shelves in the library, awakened my latent aptitude for writing.

The entertaining way in which Enid told her stories, with clarity and humour, infused me with the encouragement I needed to follow my inspirers.

In Enid's home, a far cry from my own, away from the worries and torment I was experiencing, I found it was what my grieving mind needed.

I had time on my hands in this unhurried life to pursue the things I loved to do. But, I also had an appreciative, encouraging audience in Enid that brought out the best in me.

I loved the library. I spent most of my free time thumbing through Miss Collett's collection of biographies given to her by famous actors and her friends. By the inscriptions written inside the books, it was clear they were very fond of her. I wasn't in the least surprised as I came to know her.

I did most of my writing and drawing in this pleasant reading room. Every chance I got, I used it to create pictures, scribble poems, and transcribe Enid's short stories. I had become obsessed, it seemed, with writing, even waking up in the night with my pen and paper at the ready.

27.10.1997 2:30 a.m.
Scribble
Scribble, scribble, scribble,
Scribbling all the time,
Scribbling your life on earth,
Scribbling in every line.

I was scribbling in the morning, scribbling down at night, scribbling still at the break of dawn, scribbling with all my might.
Scribbling at sunset, scribbling with glee, scribbling by the light of the moon,
And scribbling while I dream.

Scribble, scribble, scribble,
Scribbling all the time,
Scribbling your life on earth,
Scribbled in every line.

I peeled the potatoes, cut a few of the unusual yellow carrots that had grown in the kitchen garden, and put them on to boil. I had made a pie which was cooking nicely in the oven.

Opening the large pantry door, I walked through the small room and reached for the Foxes dry sherry on the shelf.

I glanced around the cold room: preservative pans, pickle jars, beautiful crockery which must have been at least one hundred years old. Jugs, huge serving plates, vegetable dishes, and large and small cheese domes, all neatly standing to attention on the marble shelves.

Everything that was ever needed in a Victorian farmhouse kitchen was here.

I quietly closed the door and checked that the dinner was ok before I left it to its own devices for a while.

I had bought Enid's usual tipple from the Co-op next door earlier that day. She wasn't a big drinker, but I always made sure there was a supply of this, as it would not have done to have had to go and buy it somewhere else if we had completely run out. As I have said, Enid was a stickler for supporting the local stores.

I got two fine-cut sherry glasses out, laid them on the tray with the bottle of sherry, and took it to where Enid was waiting in the lounge for me, setting the timer so I didn't burn the food before I did so.

I had been surprised when Enid had asked me to join her, but we were becoming good friends by now. One glass each was enough as an appetizer for dinner.

We both became engrossed in our game of scrabble that was kept in the cabinet by her chair. I loved the challenging game played with Enid; it was always a tough contest.

"It keeps the brain ticking over,"

Enid said wisely.

Sometimes, if the game was exciting and particularly lengthy, we would break off for dinner and quickly return to it after our meal. Neither of us would relent until one of us had won.

Occasionally, we would have a break from this, and she would share photographs with me instead.

Sitting close to her on the sofa, I listened with delight while she would relate what was happening at the time it was taken. I took in every detail, even things in the background, such as haystacks, carts, old shops, and clothes she was wearing, noting the difference in relation to today's fashion.

Enid would really come alive at these times. Without realizing it, she had picked up a few pointers from the actors she had worked with, or indeed, perhaps it was they who had picked up pointers from her as she directed them.

I relived every moment of her unusual life through her. I thought I would be coming to work to nurse a frail old lady, and instead, here I was, enjoying real-life plays and dramas through Enid's fascinating stories.

There were photos of her at garden parties with princesses, and there were signed books with heartfelt inscriptions from some of the world's most famous actors and actresses.

Everything for a captivating play was here at the fingertips of the quiet, sincere elderly lady I knew as Enid Marjory Collett.

Words cannot describe how much I loved being a part of her memories. If nothing else had happened in my life, I would always remember the most exciting stories she told me.

I sketched one of the photographs of the Collett children.

"We were sitting on the tree stump there."

Enid pointed to a spot in the front garden close to her front door.

"It was taken in 1910."

I remember how surprised Enid was when she saw it.

"I can recognize Ruby straight away. It is a very good likeness."

Going to work for Enid was like going to see an old friend. On taking her breakfast in bed I usually found her reading her book.

"And what have you done now?" she would ask me, smiling.

I would read out things to her, maybe read her a poem that had come to me that morning or overnight or a sketch I had drawn. She was always absorbed and used to gladly listen while eating her breakfast and drinking her coffee in bed.

She was pleased that I was taking an interest in her, writing down her memoirs, and she was always willing to share what keepsakes she had to assist me with this.

She even allowed me to take her file home with me once, to go through everything properly.

If I had known then that years later, I would be writing a full account of her life story, I would have made more notes. I could have photocopied ration books from the war, magazines from the Shows she directed, and letters from actresses. In particular, the letters from Enid's close friend Diana Morgan, Welsh Playwright who was married to a successful actor, Robert Mc Dermot. She had written to Enid for many years after she retired.

Enid had kept everything neatly filed away and was pleased to show me them all.

Even the accounts belonging to her parents, from the running of the farm.

As it was usually, when I returned home, I found some sort of catastrophe waiting for me to deal with. The photographs, letters and other interesting memorabilia were kept for when I was relaxing, which was usually when I was back at Enid's. I returned them promptly as I knew how precious they were to Enid.

I wished now that I had, at least, drawn copies of more photographs, especially the one taken outside the front door, of all four children with their father. He was holding a gun, and Ruby and Stanley were holding a couple of rabbits by their ears. You could see the look of despondency on Enid's face.

There was another picture, of Enid and a friend, in white tennis skirts and yet another, of her and her friend punting on the River Cam.

Maybe these photos are lost forever, as I have been unable to trace any close relatives who may have kept them. I fear many things belonging to the family have been lost.

The photograph that I had sketched of the Collett children in the garden, she remembered well.

"We had to sit for ages, just waiting for the cameraman to set up.

"Don't move, he had said.

I was so bored. I just couldn't see the point of us all sitting there waiting for so long. All I could think of was poor little Margot. She was only two. I couldn't understand why no one had put a bonnet on her. I was afraid she would get pneumonia."

Enid was always more concerned about her siblings than she was about herself. Especially as Margot was so young, she was afraid that her baby sister was going to become seriously ill. I noted that Enid had a gentle nature, which never seemed to leave her. She was a strong-minded, sensible woman, but she was sensitive and caring and had a genuine regard for people.

Her kindness, I noted, never seemed to wane.

I always enjoyed our meals together. It was usually spent leisurely chatting over lunch or dinner. Sometimes it was topical conversation, sometimes about days gone by.

While talking about the forces of nature one day, Enid recalled a couple of particularly memorable events. But of course, you can't get to almost a hundred years old without some amazing occurrences happening in that time.

"One such incident," Enid had told me, "was when a large red glowing object had come down about a mile away, in Woodlands Road Great Shelford.

"It was in 1978. I remember it well. It smashed all the windows facing this way."

Her eyes widened as she told me about the next surreal event.

"Another time, the same year, large icicles of over 5 inches long landed out in the street!

I remember Ruby running outside, and she picked one up. It was huge. She put it into the freezer, and kept it there for ages." ** Article in paper research 1978.

Enid spoke about her elder sister, Ruby, a lot. She sounded feisty, fearless, and full of get-up-and-go. She really brought her character alive. However, her personality it seemed, was the complete opposite of Enid's.

Enid was shy and modest. But don't be taken in by this, later on, in one of her stories, you will find out just how daring and courageous she really was.

Ruby, who Enid had told me called herself Colin, had been the head of a distinguished prep school. Her tutors must have seen how good she was at organising her classmates and therefore employed her to keep the girls under control.

Ruby was always experimenting with plants, said Enid one day when I asked her about her siblings.

I had to laugh, though, as Enid solemnly recorded this story one day.

"We were all going about our business one day as usual. I was sitting here, opening letters, and Ruby was in the kitchen doing something or other.

Suddenly, there was a huge explosion! It frightened the life out of me. I couldn't think what on earth it could be, and the noise of it shook the house. It was terrifying, and I thought we had been attacked.

But Ruby suddenly tore out of the kitchen, and was rushing down to the cellar. I hurried down behind her to see what was happening.

However, it was Ruby's huge marrow she had been nurturing for months. I didn't really know what she was doing down there. All I knew was that Ruby kept going down the cellar, to see how her marrow was getting on. She was always experimenting with plants. Consequently, I didn't take any notice of her most of the time.

It had unexpectedly blown up! There were pieces of vegetable marrow scattered all round the walls, and what was left of the ragged zucchini, was still hanging inside a net on a string suspended from the ceiling."

Enid smiled while I laughed so loud at the thought of Ruby's exploding marrow.

I had heard of this happening before when filling the marrow with brown sugar to make rum. Perhaps that was what her sister was doing.

I have been told, by ardent wine makers, that after filling a marrow with sugar, it was hung up and left to ferment. A hole is made in the bottom of the vegetable, and as it rots, it drips out pure rum.

"However, keep a careful eye on it" I was cautioned "because they have been known to blow up."

I thought of this story as I laughed.

I have never tried it, but I have been told it is delicious.

No wonder Ruby kept going down to the cellar to check on it.

Enid continued her story.

"Anyhow, as I was saying, Ruby was always interested in father's work. She was an expert with plants, and had done a lot of training. I was never really that interested in agricultural things, but I always supported Ruby."

I don't think Enid had much choice really, as Enid told me on a number of occasions how forceful Ruby was.

"Now where did I get to? Oh yes.

Well, Ruby was one of the first women agricultural inspectors in the country.

I used to go to Worcester every year with her to support her. Most people in the agricultural business were men, so Ruby was glad of my company on these occasions.

Every year, as a treat for accompanying Ruby to Worcester, she took me camping!

I wouldn't say I liked it. However, Ruby was very forceful.

I was always hungry on these excursions. We travelled for miles, mainly to Worcestershire, but once we travelled right up to Scotland."

After reading the account below, I realise now why they went to Edinburgh. Enid continued her story.

"We didn't take sandwiches or anything to eat with us. Ruby always said we would buy our food on the way.

It was much easier to go along with her than argue, but I was always hungry.

There were not many shops in Scotland, and the roads were rugged and wild.

Ruby didn't like to stop too often, so it was frequently hours before we had a break.

When we did stop, it was always in a remote place, far away from any shops.

I remember it was breathtakingly beautiful, being among the hills, but I couldn't enjoy it really, as I was constantly hungry.

We had driven for many hours, and I was glad to stop for some rest, and a little something to eat, even if it wasn't much. I was so tired; after we had put up the tent, and had a scant meal, that I fell off to sleep immediately.

At 6 am, however, when I was fast asleep, Ruby shook me awake. She was snatching up our camping gear and packing it into the car. She was in the driver's seat, waiting to go, before I was even dressed.

We had no food left for breakfast, we did not even have a cup of tea, it was miserable," said Enid.

"I hated it, but it was no use arguing with Ruby.

We had travelled for a couple of days with hardly any food, and I was so grateful to see that we eventually came to a grocery shop, where we could buy some provisions at last. I was feeling sick with hunger.

Let's stop and get some food, I suggested, but I couldn't believe it, as Ruby drove straight past, and continued down the road as fast as she could, saying, 'No, we will get some at the next shop!'

Well, as you can imagine, stores were so infrequent, we didn't see one at all that day, as I knew we wouldn't.

I remember it well. We had four slices of bread left. That was all we had, nothing else."

Poor Enid's face told the story well.

"We found a nice place to camp by a stream and put the tent up. It wasn't particularly comfortable, but it was no use complaining.

We sat on the ground, and Ruby got the bread out. 'We will eat one slice now, and keep the other piece of bread for the morning,' she said.

It was torture, I nibbled on the bread, trying to make it last. I was just so hungry by now.

Then she said 'if we go to bed now, the morning will come more quickly.'

I laid awake all night, though, I couldn't sleep for thinking about the slice of bread that I was to have for my breakfast.

When it was 6 am, Ruby suddenly jumped out of bed, and started to gather our things together and put them in the car. I was so glad it was morning when morning came, and I got up quickly. My stomach was in knots where I was so hungry. I couldn't wait to have my one slice of bread.

Then, suddenly Ruby started raking through the bag, shouting, 'oh no, the dog has eaten the bread!'

I could have cried.

It was the same every year."

Enid would have continued to go along with Ruby, even though she detested it.

They were quite different characters, I could tell. Ruby was persistent and commanding, and Enid was gentle and compliant. Both, however, had very good business skills.

I couldn't help laughing, though, as I imagined the robust strong-minded Ruby striding about in the Scottish hillside.

She was obviously a brilliantly focused businesswoman. Not afraid of hard work and had a sense of determination that took her to the top of her profession.

While researching, I came across a very interesting article written by librarian Graham Hardy. Thank you, Graham, for allowing me to re-print this in my book.

Ruby Collett was in her eighties when she made this remark to a younger neighbour. A student probationer gardener at RBGE in the 1920s, Ruby was a force of nature, and I'd like to share some of her experiences with plants. During her time at RBGE, she would learn much about propagating and tending to new and established species. This practical Ruby's full name was Ruby Sarah Martha Collett.

She was born on a large mixed farm at Abbot's Ripton, Huntingdonshire, in 1900.

Prior to arriving at RBGE in August 1924, she had garnered five years of practical experience working in private and collegiate gardens.

From 1919 to early 1922, Ruby worked as a gardener at Reading University and Loughborough College. During this time, she gained the R.H.S. Senior Certificate – 1st Class.

At Loughborough, she managed the garden and grounds of five student hostels and supervised a team of assistant lady gardeners.

J.F. Driver, Works Manager at Loughborough College, gave Ruby a recommendation for her application to RBGE, in which he states:

'Besides being a good practical gardener, Miss Collett has high theoretical qualifications and has had an excellent experience.' J. F. Driver

In 1923 Ruby started as a gardener in a private garden at Pampisford, Cambridgeshire, where she worked under glass and outdoors. Her employer was Mrs Annie Hudson, the widow of P R Hudson, a significant brewer in Cambridgeshire.

She took up her place at RBGE in the August of 1924, coming from a position at Anstey Hall, Cambridgeshire, where she was working in the glasshouses.

We know from a personal letter that she roared around Edinburgh on a motorcycle.

Ruby excelled academically, never receiving a mark below 75 per cent and in two subjects (Systematic Botany and Meteorology) passing with full marks.

When she left RBGE in February 1927, Sir William Wright Smith, Regius Keeper, noted in the certificate he issued that:

'Her work in the Royal Botanic Garden has been performed carefully, skilfully, and intelligently and her conduct has been in every respect satisfactory.'

On leaving RBGE, Ruby was the first woman to gain a position with the Ministry of Agriculture as an Assistant Inspector of Horticulture. She worked primarily among the orchards in Worcestershire.

In 1933 she re-located to Cornwall, having amassed sufficient capital to purchase a farm of eight small fields covering approximately 12 acres and two cob-walled cottages, to become a producer of good quality flowers and fruit, a long-held ambition of hers. The farm was located at Quenchwell, Perranwell, halfway between Truro and Falmouth.

In March 1934, seeds of forty-five shrubs and herbaceous plants, including Lilium regale, Ceanothus veitchianus, Spiraea douglasii, and Meconopsis wallichii, were sent to Ruby from RBGE.

Ruby wrote about her experiences during the first six years of her flower farm in an article published in the August 1939 issue of The Journal of the Ministry of Agriculture.

Before Ruby purchased her farm, she was advised to make sure the farm was saleable in the event of her failing to make good.

Undaunted, she set to work, but with a plan that every endeavour had to be made to make both buildings and equipment serve more than one purpose.

She also improved her farm by building a cottage for her foreman, improving her own cottage, and building additional storage and picking sheds, a garage, and water tanks.

As well as working on her farm herself, Ruby employed a small staff of three, took on horticultural students, and employed seasonal workers for flower harvesting.

One of the first things she tried to assess was whether mechanical or horsepower was the best way of powering work on the farm.

A rototiller won out over the horses after some trying experiences.

By 1939 the rototiller had more than paid for itself.

Ruby continued using the rototiller for four years, after which she purchased a tractor for ploughing, rolling, and harrowing.

St Brigid anemone

By 1939 the crops cultivated included over an acre of anemones, the same of daffodils, and 2 acres of strawberries, with smaller areas of violets, raspberries, blackberries, and gooseberries.

In the early years of the farm, the number of strawberry plants sold was between 50,000 to 70,000 per year, and the number of viola plants sold was between 20,000 and 50,000.

Here are a few of Ruby's observations from her article:

'I have worked up a connection for plants of high quality, which are despatched to all parts of Great Britain.

I aim at the best; there is no stinting where manures and cultivators are concerned.

I would like to emphasize the great importance of introducing the very best strains and stocks for the initial plantings.

Any success I have achieved I attribute to the experience which comes from being born on a large mixed farm, to having had a horticultural training followed by a varied practical experience, to having enjoyed good health, and to the possession of a large capacity for hard work.'

Sometime in the late 1940s, Ruby re-located within Cornwall, moving to Rosmergy, in the Parish of St. Agnes, in the Wheal Lawrence Valley, a former centre of Cornish copper-mining.

Here she established another flower farm from five fields.

Ruby's enthusiasm for plants meant that she was a very hard worker who expected more of her employees than was perhaps the norm. Someone who worked for her for a short period recalled her as a 'hard taskmaster.'

One thing that Ruby grew commercially at Rosmergy was shrubs, including Pittosporum.

Amongst the seeds sent from RBGE in 1934, were seeds of P. crassifolium and P. divaricatum.

P. crassifolium, a native of New Zealand, was particularly suited to the climate of the south-west, and has naturalised in some places in Cornwall.

Serials Librarian Graham Hardy

Royal Botanic Garden Edinburgh, 20a Inver Leith Row, Edinburgh, EH3 5LR, Scotland, UK

Pittosporum crassifolium

In a letter, Mrs Isobel Burrows, whose mother was a friend of Ruby's, describes the beauty of the garden, Ruby created around her cottage, situated only half a mile from the sea.

Ruby planted a protective shelter belt of pines, olearia, griselinia and elaeagnus, within which she grew single specimen trees such as Cornus kousa, eucalyptus, and copper beech.
In front of the cottage were a tree paeony and a flowering cherry.

Fuchsia magellanica provided an edging on one side of the drive up to the cottage.
The garden was particularly attractive in winter when camellias and Rhododendron 'Christmas Cheer' flowered.
 Gunnera planted by Ruby is remarked on by walkers in the area to this day.
A keen golfer, Ruby played the game well into her eighties. She created a practice green on part of her land, and tended it with a particular pride, offering sixpence to any child who could discover a dandelion growing on it.
Ruby reached the age of 90 but sadly died in her garden, in tragic circumstances, on Boxing Day 1990.
Anne Meredith looks in more detail at Miss Collett's experiences in her thesis 'Middle class women and horticultural education, 1890-

1939' Ph.D. University of Sussex (2001). [EThOS ID: uk.bl.ethos.390831]
My thanks are due to Mr Tom Thompson (St Agnes Museum (www.stagnesmuseum.org.uk)), Mrs Isobel Burrows, and Mr & Mrs John Branfield for providing information about Miss Collett and her garden and nursery at Rosmergy.
Written by Graham Hardy, May 2016.

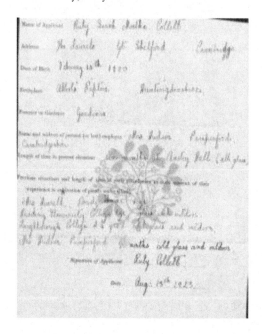

Ruby Collett Probationer Gardener Application Form

The gardening period no doubt helped develop this very formidable plant woman.

456 individuals were taken on as probationer gardeners at RBGE between 1889 and 1939. Only seven of that group (1.5 %) were women.

I am indebted to Graham Hardy, as I have been able to fill in some gaps about Ruby that I didn't know.

Nestled in the Cornish village still stands a garden nursery. On the grounds where Ruby first started off her smallholding.

On reading my notes through, Enid told me that Ruby used to grow vegetables for Covent Garden and a few shops.

"She started off with fruit and potatoes, then gradually expanded.

The taxman, however, told her she was paying out more than she was bringing in. She had been living in London at the time.

46

So, father bought her a cottage with a large garden in Cornwall.

Ruby employed a handyman and his wife to help, and had an extension built for them to live in.

When the man's wife died, he stayed on to support Ruby, who was quite old by then. She had told me; he was like a brother to her.

However, Ruby started behaving quite out of character suddenly, demanding that I build a bungalow in the corner of the field for her. I thought she was going a bit funny."

Enid looked puzzled.

"So, I invited her to come and live with me."

But then Ruby said she wanted an extension built onto the house, saying it was too small. It wasn't like Ruby at all. I couldn't understand her.

She became very agitated when I rejected her idea.

I told her I didn't see the point in this, so I refused, explaining that the house was quite adequate for just the two of us.

I didn't hear from her after that.

Shortly afterward though, the police got in touch with me, asking a lot of questions about Ruby and the handyman.

Ruby was found dead, at 10 am on Boxing day morning."

Poor Enid turned her sorrowful face to me, and I felt a lump in my throat as I realised what she was telling me.

"There had, said the police, been a garden fire, and poor Ruby was found burned to death.

A can that had contained petrol had been found by the back door, and a trail from it leading to the garden fire."

"The villagers, who knew Ruby well, had been very suspicious at the time."

She turned and looked me in the eye.

"And so was I."

A cold shiver ran down my spine.

I was sad to hear about Ruby's abysmal death. She was 89 when she came to her tragic end under these suspicious circumstances. I felt I had come to know Ruby through Enid's precise portrayal. She had brought her dynamic character alive, full of vitality and vigour. It seemed so unfair that she had fallen victim to such devastating conditions. For anyone to die in these situations is appalling, but Ruby had put so much effort into succeeding at the things she loved that I couldn't believe it.

"Even the police who had made extensive enquiries were doubtful.

Apparently, the man had been suffering from schizophrenia, but there was not enough evidence to prove he was guilty of murdering poor Ruby.

I really thought Ruby was suffering mentally when she kept insisting on a bungalow being built. After I refused, I hadn't heard from her.

Then, shortly afterward, Ruby was found dead. It was awful. There were so many police enquiries.

Margot was living here too, and a week later, they took Margot into hospital, and she died shortly afterwards. I think it must have been the shock."

Margot Collett aged 81 had left a probate of £274391. Ruby was 89 years old when she met her tragic end.

With a sigh, hands still resting neatly in her lap, Enid remarked sadly at least she went quickly.

It must have been an awful shock for her to lose both her sisters so close together. Poor Enid couldn't bear the thought of either of her siblings suffering.

CHAPTER SEVEN

"I wonder if there is an afterlife?" Enid was considering one day as we were having lunch. "I have been thinking a lot about my brother Stanley lately. He was in the RAF, you know. It seems strange that I am the only survivor of all of us."

"How long has it been?" I asked.

"Oh, he passed away years ago (1980)," Enid replied, answering my question. "He would have been 98 next week. Now there is just me. I don't suppose it will be long before I join them," she said wistfully. "It would be nice to think that perhaps one day we would all meet up again. It's a shame that after spending considerable time in the RAF that he died with problems of the throat caused by his time in the RAF."

Then after a brief pause, she continued, "I am the sole survivor of all of us now. As we have no known relatives, I will have to think carefully about where I shall leave the bulk family money," she added wistfully.

This must have been a constant weight for her to bear. She spoke about the problem quite often. I could not comment on it in my position, only to suggest certain charities. I had no idea of the size of her estate, nor would I ask.

Then, as an afterthought, as if answering my silence and unasked question, Enid pulled herself up in her chair, hands still folded in her lap. "I never heard my mother or father talk about money. I don't know how they got it or what they did with it. All I know is that I got 6d a week in pocket money. I would buy a halfpenny-worth of sweets each week from the village shop. The newsagent and sweetshop are still there, in the same place."

She seemed to trail off, perhaps lost in her imagination. Then as she came to, she said, "Now, where did I get to?... Oh yes. Before I was quite grown up, my aunt left me a house, in Peterborough, in her will."

She sat bolt upright now, folded hands gracefully in her lap, staring ahead of her. I continued eating my soup, relieved that she was telling me another story, as I felt unqualified to speak to her about the subject of money. I waited for her to gather her thoughts, knowing another good story was coming. Enid was sensitive, so I am sure she knew this, and she moved on effortlessly, and after a gentle prompt from me, she continued her story.

"Ah yes, well, when my aunt died, she left me a house in Peterborough. It brought me £30 a year in rent money. I was still quite young when I inherited it, and I was supposed to use the money to buy clothes. However, I wasn't wildly excited about clothes. As long as I was smart and dressed sensibly for the weather, that was all I was worried about."

I remembered comparing Enid to myself at that age. Money was very hard to come by for me. Just trying to keep myself smart was difficult. I would have loved to have had an allowance like this. I loved clothes and fashion.

"I suppose," Enid said thoughtfully, "that I must have rented it out for about twenty years. However, it started to sink, and I had to go to see my tenant about it. So, I travelled to Peterborough in the hope of remedying the problem. I looked around as I waited for her to answer the door. It was a nice little cottage with a pretty, well-stocked garden."

Enid paused and smiled suddenly. I smiled, too, curiously, waiting for her to finish.

She continued, "After a while, my tenant opened the door and invited me in. Well, I was so astonished; the floor had sunk so badly, it was like walking uphill. The woman who was living there had put bricks under the table legs so the crockery didn't slide off the table. There were even bricks under the chair legs. It made me feel quite dizzy looking at it," Enid said, stifling a giggle.

We laughed heartily, as I had said she could have charged people to go in as they do at fairgrounds, to enter The Crooked House.

"So, I thought it was time to sell it," Enid finished after our bout of laughter had subsided.

Another week over; time was flying by so quickly at Enid's. There was always another story to hear. It was better than going to the theatre, I had thought. I returned home, once again, refreshed and positive. The week at home soon went by, and I was again back with Enid, waiting for the next episode of her memoirs.

In 1920, Enid had left school, and it was time to start thinking about what she was going to do now.

"There were not a lot of choices for girls career-wise," said Enid. "It was either become a school teacher, nurse, or secretary. I was not too fond of the idea of doing any of these things. However, I had to do something, so out of the three choices, I decided to enrol in a secretarial course at Reading University. As I was nearing the completion of the course, I was recommended to attend an interview for a post at The Festival Theatre in Cambridge.

"So, early one morning, I rode into Cambridge on my bicycle, not really relishing the thought of an interview. After climbing the stairs to the proprietor's office, I sat down opposite Mr Gray. He seemed a nice enough man, but I was shocked when my interviewer asked if I wanted to go on the stage. It was the only question he asked me. I had difficulty understanding him at first because he had a terrible stammer. But when I realised he was actually asking me if I wanted to perform on the stage, I was horrified, thinking it might be a requirement.

"'Certainly not,' I replied with such vehement that he actually laughed."

I laughed too. Poor shrinking Enid would rather have hidden under the stage than be on it.

"The delighted Terrance Gray said at once, 'You've got the job. So that was that.' I think he had become quite fed up with girls, applying for the post, with a secret ambition of becoming an actress in the future," said Enid.

She had gone half-heartedly to the interview with Mr Terrance Gray, who had recently bought the theatre. It never occurred to Enid that fate had planted her feet on the pathway of a long and satisfying career.

Enid was a shy, quiet woman; even now, she was in her twilight years; I cannot imagine she would have liked being exposed to crowds of people. However, she was also a very conscientious woman who, throughout her career in the theatre world, always gave 110 per cent. Every day Enid rode her bicycle the 4 miles into Cambridge and back home again when her work was finished.

"It was quite safe in those days as there were very few cars around."

She started her career doing menial tasks, such as making tea, writing letters, and filing. However, as time went on and the theatre was ready to put on shows, it became apparent that Enid was much more useful to Mr Gray than he had imagined.

"He had spent thousands of pounds doing up the old theatre in Barnwell Road Cambridge. It was quite spectacular."

CHAPTER EIGHT
TERRANCE GRAY HAROLD RIDGE AND THE FESTIVAL THEATRE

A typical programme for a year, at the height of The Festival Theatres success, divided into three seasons of eight weeks in 1928.

Jan.16th	Caesar and Cleopatra	Bernard Shaw
Jan. 23rd	Inheritors...........................	Susan Glaspell
Jan.30th	The Carthaginian....................	Frank Taylor
Feb.6th	From Morn to Midnight	George Kaiser
Feb.13th	Cheezo	Lord Dunsany
	Dr Knock...........................	Jules Romains
Feb.20th	Richard 111.........................	Shakespeare
Feb.27th	The Passion Flower.................	Jacinto Benevente
Mar. 5th	The knight of the Burning Pestle....	Beaumont and Fletcher
Apr. 23rd	The Pretenders......................	Henrik Ibsen
Apr.30th	The Devils Disciple.................	Bernard Shaw
May 7th	The Riding to Lithend...............	Gordon Bottomley
	A Royal Audience....................	Terrance Gray
May 14th	The Last Hour.......................	George Gravely
	The Dreamy Kid.....................	Eugene O'Neill
	Emperor Jones......................	Eugene O'Neill
May 21st	Madame Pepita......................	Martinez Sierra
May 28th	Adam the Creator....................	Karel and Josef Kapek
June 4th	The Birds...........................	Aristophanes
Oct. 10th	Heartbreak House....................	Bernard Shaw
Oct. 22nd	The man who ate the Popomack	W. J. Turner
Oct. 29th	The Show............................	John Galsworthy
Nov. 5th	The Subway..........................	Elmer Rice
Nov. 12th	As You Like It.......................	Shakespeare
Nov. 19th	The Spook Sonata....................	Strindberg
Nov. 26th	The Hairy Ape.......................	Eugene O'Neill

Terrance Gray's severe speech impediment was a hindrance when it came to directing plays. He had great difficulty in conveying his instructions to the actors and actresses. Enid's talents went far beyond that of secretary, as she knew how to decipher what Terrance Gray was trying to say.

"He got very frustrated when the actors couldn't understand what he was saying. I understood him perfectly," said Enid, "so I used to tell the actors what he wanted them to do. It was simple enough."

Enid didn't know how valuable she had become, as Mr Gray started to direct all the performances through her. It must have been a huge relief to him.

The once boring job of secretary had taken a turn for the better, and from then on, life was never the same again for Enid. She quietly got on with her role as a personal secretary, interpreter, and unintended director.

The mild, unaffected Enid was now meeting vibrant, exhilarating artists from all walks of life. Not just directing them, but through her work, she was becoming a supporter and friend to many.

Besides fraternising with famous actors, she encountered fresh raw talent, those who were on their first steps into the entertainment industry.

"I was meeting some very influential people at The Festival and was enjoying my work much more than I had first thought conceivable."

Enid appreciated the brilliance, of documented playwrights, such as Noel Coward and George Bernard Shaw for example, and watched and learned from gifted directors, such as Peter Godfrey and Norman Marshall. She worked conscientiously with an enthusiasm that the noble Terrance respected, but couldn't help taking advantage of, for Enid looked up the unconventional Terrance Gray and his fanciful ways. He couldn't possibly go wrong, and her passion for her work encouraged him all the way.

Enid had a rare supportive quality; she was Mr Gray's employee and was faithful and dependable to the end. Her business relationship with her employer, over the years, became invincible. The fresh, unique theatre was just what the public needed, thought Enid.

Terrance James Stannus Gray, 1895-1986, was of noble birth and was the only son of Anglo-Irish Sir Harold William Stannus Gray, 1867-1951, and Lady Rowena Dorothea Elizabeth Gray. The two were cousins when they married and had come over from Northern Ireland to live in the Seaside town of Felixstowe in Suffolk.

It was here that Terrance was born on 14th September 1895. He attended school at Ascham St. Vincent's. in Eastbourne, where he received a thorough education. From there, he went on to Eton and Oxford University. His Aristocratic parents had bought the house at Gog Magog Hills Estate, Cambridge, when they came over from Ireland in the early 20th century. They lived there until their death in the 1950s.

His parents owned a vineyard in France, which Terrance took charge of after the collapse of the Festival Theatre. He also took care of the family's racehorses in Ireland, and his horse Zarathustra won the Ascot Gold Cup in 1956. It was ridden by the renowned Lester Piggott.

Terrance Gray was tall and good-looking, and he always dressed distinctively. He wore a broad-brimmed hat and sported a striking beard. It was said he could be seen sauntering in the streets of Cambridge on many a day. He was educated at Eton for two years and at Magdalene College in Cambridge for one year before the war broke out. Prior to his interest in the theatre, Terrance Gray had been an ambulance driver for the Red Cross in France and Italy during the 1914-1918 war. He had also been an air mechanic in the first world war for the Royal Flying Corps.

Although he was a man of many achievements, he was a very private person. He was a relatively shy man, and it was noted that he preferred to hide behind masks. In this way, he was a bit like Enid, who always tried to keep out of the limelight throughout her lifetime. Maybe that is why she understood him so well; they were two of a kind.

The old Barnwell Theatre Royal in Cambridge was in a pitiful state in 1926. It had been reduced from its former glory to a crumbling mess when Terrance had seen it. However, he had seen the potential in the dilapidated building, and he and Harold Ridge had taken on the challenge of restoring it. Terrance had thought it an awful waste, and he had come up with the idea of recreating it into something magnificently spectacular.

Terence Gray and Harold Ridge, his founding partner, were not professional men of the Theatre. However, both were remarkably talented. Thirty-year-old Terrance Gray was an Egyptologist, and Harold Ridge was a metallurgical engineer. It seemed an unlikely partnership to venture into theatre production. Nevertheless, it worked. Harold Ridge, Terrance Gray's founding partner, was an expert in the new electric lighting and took care of the extravagantly designed illumination of the stage. He had the ability to make a scene look dramatic and stunning, using Schwabe flood lighting and plaster cyclorama, to create the illusion of sky, open space, or distance, changing it accordingly to the play being shown at the time. Not only was he an excellent electrician, but he was also a gifted amateur actor and writer and published the invaluable book *Stage Lighting for Little Theatres*, which was successfully sold all over the country.

A major accomplishment of his was the provision of the lighting for Shakespeare's New Memorial Theatre at Stratford. The old Memorial Theatre had burned down in 1926 and rebuilt in 1930. It was a huge confidence boost for Ridge. From this point, Harold Ridge went on to be a leading authority on stage lighting in England. However, it was in the Festival theatre that he was able to try out all his new ideas initially. It was an important period in history for the Theatre. Terrance was full of new concepts, some inspired by his interest in Egyptology and Greek mythology. Terrance Gray's great love of Egyptology revealed itself in the dramatic production of the Oresteia Trilogy. It was performed on an open stage, and of course, Harold Ridge provided the electric lighting.

It was one of the most memorable and greatest of these plays that The Festival Theatre had enjoyed in its time. It was a huge success with the famous Irish-born Ninnette de Valois (1898-2001) choreographing and a group of other highly talented people responsible for music, costumes, and masks. Ninnette de Valois was a dancer, teacher, choreographer, and director of classical ballet in the 1920s. Many of the Royal Ballet performances can be traced back to her influence as a choreographer, and she probably owes their success to her.

The cast was headed by Maurice Evans, Miriam Lewis, and Hedley Briggs. Indeed, in his book, *The Other Theatre*, Norman Marshall said that it is one of the most magnificently successful productions I have ever seen. Terrance was determined to have the finest money they could buy for the theatre. Nothing less would do. He extravagantly poured an abundance of cash into various equipment for the stage, luxurious seating for the auditorium, and lavish decoration on the walls and ceilings. He wanted people to feel special when they walked into the building, relaxing in the restaurant with good food and wine of the best quality. He wanted them to bathe in the luxury of the comfortable seating, providing ease that had never been known in a playhouse in this country before.

His strategy was to present each play in a completely unique manner, with Enid at his side, to construe his words and instructions to the actors and actresses. People were astonished on 22nd November 1926 when the Festival opened its doors; it was clear that Terrance Gray was not going to go along with the traditional way of producing plays. Give people what they needed, he had thought. He shunned the ordinary, traditional ways that plays were presented at the time.

In Norman Marshall's book, The Other Theatre, he was quoted to have said about the old way of presenting plays. *They are playing the old game of illusion and glamour and all the rest of the 19th-century hocus pocus and bamboozle.* Terrance Gray worked relentlessly in the transformation of The Festival Theatre with the loyal, hardworking Enid by his side. He provided a service that was the best you could find anywhere in England in the late1920s. He wanted to change people's experience of the outdated theatre, and he certainly did.

He was a man who cared about humanity, and the prices in the restaurant were deliberately kept low, mainly for students. He was noted to have said that he wanted undergraduates to drink responsibly. The fine wines probably came from the family's vineyard in France. It was said you could buy a pitcher of quality wine for one and sixpence, a price that could not be matched for the quality anywhere in England.

Certainly, at that time of day, even in London, such superiority and choice were hard to find. Terrance was particularly innovative in his highly original ideas. With a completely diverse perspective, he was audacious enough to carry them out from the present-day production of plays. He experimented on stage settings, saying that people didn't need all the old-fashioned paraphernalia used in plays of the day. He preferred to have the plays performed on a virtually empty stage. The ornate steps, ramps, and a turntable that took centre stage were solidly built and looked spectacular. Used in place of normal stage props, the effect transformed the stage into a surreal podium. Unlike anything seen in England before.

"Terrance Gray spent a great deal of money, you know, on the set-up. Luckily enough, he was able to do this. He must have thought he would recuperate this eventually," said Enid reflectively. "Another idea that he adopted was that you couldn't tell where the stage ended and the auditorium began. It was exactly how he had planned it. He wanted the audience to be a part of the actual plays, to experience the transformation in a completely different way, without the usual props. He said they weren't needed as it was an insult to intelligence."

I supposed he meant that it was a bit like canned laughter; in other words, you have to be told when to laugh, as you just don't get the joke. However, the country was probably, not ready for the pioneering impresario's innovative initiation. Today, this would be nothing particularly out of the ordinary; in fact, currently, people think it is a clever interaction with the audience. Nonetheless, it took years for this way of producing plays to eventually become popular; the public could not accept Terrance's way-out ideas at that time.

***

As a new theatre owner and entrepreneur, Terrace Gray had the advantage of being rich, and it showed in the sumptuous set-up for the theatre-goer.

"He wanted people to have a unique social experience that set itself apart from anything they had ever known before," Enid relived the theatre as she showed me her keepsakes.

It was a place to devour exquisite food, and good wines, all in the luxury of plush comfortable seats. You could see the transformation of people's worried faces as they relaxed into a state of calm expectation. It was something virtually unheard of at any theatre at that time of day. Usually, theatres were cheaply rented abandoned buildings, dimly lit and downright dangerous in some playhouses. Perched on the edge of a rickety chair, you crept in very often before the play finished because it was so uncomfortable.

The Theatre Royal, in Barnwell, Newmarket Road, Cambridge, was built in 1816. It had been purpose-built as a working theatre. Now, it had fallen into disrepair and was being used for purposes of all kinds other than shows. It had enjoyed prosperity from the successful plays that its fine and famous actors of the day had produced there. However, it fell on hard times and closed in the late 19th century.

From then on, it had been used for many different purposes, the most renowned being a mission hall that was proud to provide Tea and Buns for 500. As the aristocrat sauntered the streets of Cambridge, an idea had transfixed itself into the great philosopher's mind. The old theatre looked sad in its present condition. It was waiting for new energy to be instilled into its crumbling walls. Terrance Gray saw in the old building what he, and maybe the undergraduates of Cambridge, had been looking for.

He had seized the opportunity to return the theatre to its former glory in a way that the ordinary person could not have imagined. His artistic flair had given theatre-goers a new perspective on-stage performance. One that was not always received wholeheartedly. Delighted critics were kept ecstatically busy with their reports of Mr Gray's moves and fantastic concepts. One critic describes it as

"The only consistently experimental playhouse in the country."

Terrance's new diverse ideas were awe-inspiring. Talented students were hungry for the sophisticated way in which Terrance Gray presented his plays. Mr. Gray was rich and could give the people what their soul was craving for. Many people desired and thrived on the creation of the presentation. The quality of the handpicked actors and actresses, some unknown at the time, brought vast success to the stage. Enid was at the hub of everything, working in partnership with Terrance Gray to revolutionise the theatre world.

"It was terribly exciting and totally new to me."

Enid had an undiscovered talent that had laid dormant until now. Without her, The Festival Theatre, may not have even gotten off the ground. As it was, she had interpreted Gray's instructions, counted out the wages for the actors, and was a great negotiator between Mr Gray and the thespians. Everyone had soon grown to come to trust and have confidence in her. Yet Enid thought nothing of these extra duties as a secretary. She didn't realise what a great asset she had become.

The Festival Inspired many undergraduates, into a diverse state of achievement, in a ground-breaking way. It gave rise to discussions and reflections, bringing depth to their studies while leisurely bathing in the comfort and luxury, just as Mr Gray had planned it. Terrance Gray was providing what he thought had been missing in the town of Cambridge. His choice of sophisticated Shakespearian plays, at a price that even the students could afford, was a welcome gift for Cambridge and its colleges. The country was about to experience the stage in a totally brand-new way.

"People don't want to play visual make-believe," he was heard to say.

He used a technique that had never been known in the theatre world. He did away with props that were normally used, saying the "modern theatre is weary of naturalism," dubbing it as "superficial and limiting." He gave vent to his uninhabited ideas, giving the old building a new lease on life.

Late November 1926, in Newmarket Road Cambridge, Terrance Gray and his founding partner, Harold Ridge, had presented to the world a new phase for stage, and The Festival Theatre was born. He wanted the theatre-goer to have the most unforgettable, pleasurable experience that anyone had ever had before. It was certainly different from all other Theatres in England at that time. Most theatres in the early nineteen twenties had to make do with what they could acquire for venues. Usually, they were coarse, uncomfortable seating, and poorly lit.

Mr Gray, on the other hand, had had a good start with the old Barnwell Theatre. It provided a good foundation for the new well-appointed Festival

Theatre. The benefit of owning a Theatre, that had been built for the production of plays, and of course, being rich was an advantage too. He was one of the wealthiest Theatre companies in England. No expense was spared. Nothing was too good for his luxurious theatre. Terrance was determined to make it the best it could be. It was unheard of at that time.

He worked hard, and before long, The Festival theatre had now become a well-appointed venue full of comfort and luxury. His accomplishments had a significant effect on the layout of the stage settings and the production of successful plays. Terrance was now providing what he thought had been missing in the town of Cambridge. The Festival Theatre had at first seemed that it was going to be a great success. If the accomplishment could have been maintained for the duration of his reign in the Festival, it may have gone on to become one of the best theatres in the world. However, the eccentric Mr Gray's lack of leadership and unnegotiable manner of his ideas caused controversy among the producers.

Frustrated, three of the most important contributors, Harold Ridge, Norman Marshall, and the producer of Oresteia, Herbert Prentice, had left the company by the end of the year, leaving the stubborn Terrance to his impracticable ideas. It had left Terrance in a predicament, but undeterred, he had continued to produce the plays himself, with Enid as his interpreter. During the rest of his time producing in the Festival, he occasionally employed guest producers Norman Marshall and Peter Godfrey. As Norman Marshall had said, if the initial success had been maintained, it could have been one of England's most significant theatres. However, after the initial triumphs, it seemed he had other things on his mind that would eventually take over.

***

Meanwhile, the ever-faithful Enid stayed true to Terrance, and her duties went far beyond that of mere secretary. I was amazed to hear about Enid's enthralling adventures in the theatre world. It seemed to me that she had not led the quiet life I had at first supposed. Indeed, her life had been that of an adventurous soul, of whom her career took her all over the world, fraternising with many famous people along the way.

Enid kept me absorbed in her stories about her life. I never knew what was in store for me when I went back to my work after my break at home.

"Over the years, I became very good friends with Terrance Gray," Enid started one day after soup. "I loved my work and found it all very exciting. There was always something new going on. I became very good friends with Terrance. This is a picture of us at a garden party in Monaco."

She showed me all sorts of memorabilia too. It's a pity all these photos that I was shown are lost. I fear never to be found again. Enid continued her fascinating story about Terrance Gray, whom she had come to know very well over the years.

"Terrance lived in the Gog Magog Hills, you know," she started to say one day when I was enquiring where I should take a walk that afternoon. My interest was stirred once again, and with this encouragement, she continued.

His unmarried daughter lived at the Gog Magog house alone for years, Enid continued. Sadly, it was said she had no friends or visitors. When Terrance Gray married Russian noblewoman Rimsky-Korsakov, they went to live in Kensington, Queens Park Road.

"The house was full of beautiful antique furniture, some of it dating as far back as the 17th century. It had been part of the aristocrat's heritage, brought over from Ireland," Enid said.

I laughed when she continued, "The wife had said she's not going to live with a lot of old junk, so they divorced. They had been married for just one day! So, Terrance didn't see her anymore. He had, however, the good fortune to meet and marry a very nice Russian girl." said Enid. "They went to live in Monaco."

Later that day, Enid showed me a lovely photo of herself and the couple, in Monaco, at a garden party. The very nice Russian girl, incidentally, I found out, was a Russian princess from Georgia. Natalie Margaret Imertinsky. Enid told me that the eccentric Terrance Gray had left the Wandlebury Estate to The Cambridge Preservation Society for the enjoyment of the people.

"They were not supposed to build on it," she told me with a scornful look. "It came with the Proviso that it should never be built upon. There is a plaque in the grounds acknowledging his wishes."

When Terrance Gray died, he left the house and land at Wandlebury, to the Cambridge Preservation Society, in his will. The proviso was that they should not pull the house down. In six months, they had demolished it! I could see she didn't approve of this at all.

"It's now a tourist attraction," she said, "with as many as 5,000 visitors a day. It still has the same warden, and he says that the tourists are wearing away the pathways!"

Our conversations were becoming more interesting by the day. I never knew what delights Enid was going to come up with next. We finished our nutritious homemade soup, the usual Cotswold cheese, and a fresh slice of buttered bread. I tidied away while Enid retired to her lounge, turning over the things she had told me in my mind. I made a mental note to go and visit the Gog Magog hills that afternoon in the autumn of 1994.

I was amazed when I drove through the iron gates to the car park. Stories of the Grays and the actors and actresses were going around in my head as I pulled up. I looked around the area. It was vast. I never dreamed it would be so big. I have since spent many happy hours wandering through the peaceful surroundings of the Wandlebury estate, my beloved Yorkshire terrier cross by my side. I still visit, imagining how it was when the Grays lived here. However, it goes back way further than these times. As suggested by the name of The Gog Magog Hills, the area goes back as far as Anglo Saxon and Roman times.

This Photo by Unknown Author is licensed under *CC BY-SA-NC*

Wendy Clark has written a most informative and interesting book called, *Once Around Wandlebury*. I would highly recommend it to anyone who is interested in history and preservation.

CHAPTER NINE

It became apparent, after several years, that Terrance Gray was beginning to accept that the world was not ready or interested in his ideas. He became weary of the theatre, which was invariably taken over at these times by Norman Marshall and Peter Godfrey, who was director of The Gate Theatre London. Enid stayed loyal to the end.

Even after amalgamating with The Gate Theatre in London, it was blatantly obvious that his time in the theatre world was done.

Terrance had moved on. His time at the theatre was complete, and he increasingly spent more time studying the spiritual arts. He wrote books under the pseudonym of wei wu wei, a clear indication of his interest in Zen practices and their philosophies, and many people began to look at him as a sage. In June 1933, he wrote an open letter as follows: -

On 17th June, the theatre will have completed seven years of work and will cease to exist as the Festival.

"Formed by Harold Ridge and myself in 1926, contrary to the prophecy of all the theatrical people consulted, the theatre prospered from the first.

Cambridge has supported our work magnificently, for we have compromised with none and pandered to nobody's prejudices. Whatever we believe to contain truth and to be worth saying or doing, we have said or done without hesitation; for a theatre that considers everybody's feeling, seeks to please all, and offends none, will get nowhere, for it can have no policy.

What will become of the theatre I cannot say. It belongs to a company of disinterested persons for whom I managed it. I have told the company that I have done all the work I wish to do, have devoted to The Festival theatre as much of my life as I intend to devote, and that on the 17th of June I withdraw.

Perhaps the Festival will become what is termed a provincial repertory theatre. Perhaps some enterprising person will use it for establishing high-class films as I have used it for drama of a similar kind; perhaps it will become just an ordinary cinema, a nonstop variety house, a cabaret hall, a skating rink. Its future lies open to any man of enterprise, and it should prosper, for it has tradition and is a good place.

"Terrance Gray"

An open letter from the undergraduate papers read: -

"You have provided the undergraduate with \ a haven of refreshment from the banalities of the conventional stage. You have supplied the thinking man with endless food for thought, the critic with endless material for criticism, and the disputant with much weighty matter for discussion. The artist, you have supplied with inspiration; the journalist with copy; to the babbler, you have given subject for decent conversation and to the philistine a target at which to scoff." Enid worked relentlessly for the proprietor for the whole duration of The Festival Theatres life.

Terrance Gray returned to his former love of running the family's Vineyard at Tain l'Hermitage.

Amazingly, The Festival Theatre is now, after all these years, a Buddhist Centre. A Centre Terrance Gray would surely have been proud of. After all, it was his love of the spiritual way of life that sustained him in his most difficult times. He wrote eight books, in fact, on such topics in a Zen manner.

- Open Secret
- The Tenth Man
- Posthumous pieces
- Fingers pointing to the moon
- Ask The Awakened
- The Tenth Man
- Why Lazarus Laughed
- Unworldly Wise

After the closure of the Festival Theatre, Terrance travelled throughout Asia, spending a considerable amount of time in The Ashram of Ramanesh.

I am sure that Terrance Gray would have been very much at home in The Buddhist Centre in Newmarket Road Cambridge. The inside of the splendid Theatre is still as spectacular as ever.

Now a thriving Centre for Meditation, Mindfulness, Tai Chi, and Yoga brings much-needed stress relief for the many inhabitants of the city of Cambridge. An excellent bookshop and a beautiful tea room are also in the Centre. In a city with 31 Universities in it, I am sure it gives great service to those in need of relief from the stresses of life. Enid and Terrance Gray stayed friends long after he retired.

Terrance James Stannus Gray died on the 5th January in Monaco in 1987, aged 93 years old.

CHAPTER TEN

During Enid's time at The Festival Theatre, she met many influential people. One such person was Anmer Hall.

Surely that wasn't his real name, I had asked.

"Oh no," she had smiled.

"His real name was Alderson Burrell Horne. He was working under the pseudonym of Anmer Hall, where he was born.

He was a very rich man, you know." She ruminated, raising her eyebrows.

Alderson Burrell Horne was the son of Edgar Horne. Born in 1863, he was educated at Westminster School from 1876 to 1880. Then he entered Pembroke College, Oxford, in 1884.

Anmer Hall had been a successful solicitor before taking over The Festival Theatre.

He had had the imposing Ditton House, near Balcombe in Sussex, built in 1904, and Enid had been thrilled to have been invited to spend the weekend there.

Enid had a faraway look in her eyes as she continued her story.

Immediately, I was transported back to long ago, to her amazing world of mystery and splendour.

"As the new director of The Festival Theatre, he had asked me to come and stay. He lived in a great hall where you drove right up to the huge front door," she continued. "You left all your luggage in the car, and it was then taken by the footman, who would drive it away and unload it for you.

I remember that my brother Stanley had come with me on this occasion.

He would stay for a night, then go to my sister Ruby's smallholding in Cornwall.

It made sense for him to drive me to the house, then he could take the car down to Ruby's.

She had asked him to take father's bug destroyer from the farm, as she had been having some trouble with her vegetables.

I can recall," said Enid with a twinkle in her eye, "that we were shown to our rooms after Stanley and I had been welcomed with some warming coffee.

It was all very grand," she said.

"Anyhow, when I was shown to my room, all my luggage was there waiting for me.

I opened the wardrobe in the stately bedroom and was brought rapidly down to earth," she said.

"There, before me, hung all my old furs, falling away at the seams."

Enid shuffled up in her chair before continuing. I could see she was enjoying the story immensely. I laughed.

"I was horrified! And, as if that wasn't bad enough! The footman had also found the father's pesticide. Stanley was stunned when he saw the large can standing on top of the dressing table in all its glory.

I had an Austin 7 in those days." Enid continued. "It had a hood on the top of it, which could be pulled across if it was raining. The sides were open, and it was very cold in the winter. Of course, there were no heaters in the cars then, but I used to keep my old fur coats in the vehicle. Those that had seen better days, you know, the sort of thing. They were just strips of fur, really, but very welcome on a winter's day."

We laughed together as I could see the young Enid, in her elation, was brought crashing down to earth with a bang.

After a pause for a thought, she took another mouthful of the nutritious home-made soup.

I always enjoyed our meals together and spent leisurely chatting, sometimes topical, sometimes over the days gone by. You could be sure, however, whatever the subject of the conversation, it was always an interesting discussion.

Enid smiled to herself as if remembering something else.

"My brother Stanley and I had both been looking forward to the holiday.

As I said, Anmer Hall was a very rich man.

The thing I most remember was that Ditton House had a real tennis court.

Most people had a lawn tennis pitch, but tennis is something quite different.

He also had a Croquet Lawn, and after dinner, we retired to play billiards in the billiards room. It was magnificent."

She had been really impressed, but I could imagine Enid would have been as cool and professional as only she could be under such circumstances.

Enid had been a real society girl, but without any of the swank, she just wouldn't know how to brag.

We finished our soup, followed by the usual Cotswold cheese, bread and butter, and a glass of refreshing water.

"Well?" asked Enid, "What are your plans for this afternoon?

Back to today and the present, I told her I would take my usual walk.

"And where will you go?" she asked again.

When I told her I was not sure, she pushed her hands against the table and leaned back in her chair.

I soon learned that Enid was a mine of information on the village and footpaths,

"You could take the path down by the recreation ground," she offered, "Walk along by the river and through the wood, and you will come out into Woodlands Road. Then turn immediately left, and you will find yourself back on the road to Shelford.

Well, I thought, who needed an Ordnance Survey Map when you had Enid!

She had many suggestions for walks like this for me, and when I had finished jotting down her memoirs, I would go and explore the ancient footpaths that she knew so well.

I would turn over the stories that Enid had told me in my mind.

Living through her eyes, the experiences, the excitement of another time, in another world was so vast from the one I knew. I felt privileged that she had been able to share with me, in such detail, the life and times of her fascinating life.

Nature, if left alone, never changes. Of course, time changes people, but there is something comforting in knowing that the countryside, the trees, and the wild flowers stay exactly the same.

I know that when Enid walked the same footpaths as a young girl, they looked exactly the same now as they did then as I meandered along the quiet lanes.

Another week at home, and I returned ready to move into a different world again, into Enid's country home.

The library, by far my favourite place in the house and seldom used by Enid in those days, was the perfect place for me to get lost in my writing and art. When I arose in the morning, it was the first room I went to. Sipping my morning cup of tea and overlooking the enormous garden full of trees, I would sit in the stillness, bathing in the peace and splendour of nature. One morning as I sat, my mind was in a semi-trance-like state. The birds were singing sweetly, and I noticed a squirrel at the base of the tree chewing intently on some nuts. Suddenly he stopped and listened. To me nothing had broken the silence, but suddenly he leaped so high he landed on a branch halfway up the huge trunk. I sat and watched from the antique chair I was sitting in. It was then I noticed a fox standing low a few feet away.

The sun was just rising, and the scene opened before me. I thought how clever that little chap was to have instinctively known the fox was there, ready to pounce.

It was at times like this that I found to keep a pencil and paper close to hand was beneficial. Straight away, I started to write the poem that you see on the opposite page.

Other times I had no inspiration at all, but rather would wake from a dream, in the night or early morning, with just two lines from a poem playing on my mind repeatedly until I scribbled them down.

One morning I had awoken at 6 am, and while making my tea, I had words that I couldn't stop saying. It's like a song you keep singing sometimes, not knowing why.

I quickly scribbled them down. They were:

Gentle breezes softly slumber,
'Neath the Sunkissed earth.
Stay with me, my love, forever,
Let this be our birth.

While I was drinking my tea, the rest of the poem came.

My Immortal Beloved (The story of Romeo and Juliet)

That first tender kiss stirring within,
A passion that burns so deep.
It pulls the strings of two fragile young hearts,
Awakening them from sleep.

Sweet, tender love continues its journey,
The victims will ne'er be the same.
Pulling them here this way then that,
As the blood courses through their veins.

As the flame lingers longer,
The plot grows stronger.
As the vows they solemnly make,
Their secret desire adds fuel to their fire.
Each other they'll never forsake.

While their love turns to lust,
A feudal mistrust destroys what they have found.
So, while anger rises, Juliet disguises,
Her body beneath the ground.

It saves her from spending a life full of woe,
Shackled to another.
But as the plot thickens,
What she doesn't know is the banishing of her lover.

When Romeo hears of his love's supposed death,
Sweet poison he renders to take.
For life without her unbearable seems,
Never thinking of such a mistake.

With tears in his eyes, a promise to stay,
Eternally for all time.
A last tender kiss, his head on her breast,
He dies while still in his prime.

As she opens her eyes and sees what has passed,
The pain she can bear no longer.
Lifting the dagger high in the air,
She buries it deep inside her chest.

(This was where the words fitted in, in the middle of the poem)

Gentle breezes softly slumber,
Neath the sun-kissed earth.
Stay with me, my love, forever
Let this be our birth.

This pain I feel for just a moment,
Ripping out my heart.
Is not as bad as life without you,
We must never part.

Beyond my love, we now find freedom,
Lasting love forever.
The only way our love can be,
Is to die together.

As I feel the blade go deeper,
I relish in the pain.
My shallow breath is growing weaker,
As we meet again.

I slipped it into my pocket and took it into the library while I leisurely and gradually began to wake up. However, I soon started writing again as more words began streaming through my mind. As I was halfway down the page, I found that the metre changed, and the words I had jotted down earlier perfectly fit in with the prose. So I continued scribbling down my thoughts while I sipped my tea and ate my breakfast.

I never ceased to be amazed at these times. The words that I heard on waking had fitted naturally into the poem halfway through, changing the metre at the same time.

I could only put it down to the fact that I was surrounded by books of many talented actors, actresses, and the like, and maybe the energies somehow had penetrated into my thoughts and caused me to be producing poems and writing.

After I had prepared dinner that evening, instead of playing our usual game of scrabble, Enid showed me her photographs of Anmer Hall and told me how much she had enjoyed her stay there. It was there she met Tyrone Guthrie, who the new owner of the Festival had brought in as resident director.

Alderson Burrell Horne was born in 1863 in Anmer Hall. He died on 22nd December 1953, aged 90 years.

He was educated at Westminster before entering Pembrooke College in Oxford in 1884. He had been involved in World War 1 in entertainment for the troops and supported Nigel Playfair's takeover of The Lyrics Theatre in 1918.

He was now the manager at The Festival Theatre in Cambridge, and Enid was delighted at his offer for her to go and stay.

"It was all rather impressive, you know."

Enid had said one day, as we were chatting in our usual place at the farmhouse table, feasting on the deliciously home-made soup. I listened intently, even though, at the time, I hadn't realised just how outstanding it had all been!

Enid had a way of understating even the grandest of things and people she had come to know. She told her stories simply, with not a hint of self-importance.

"There were, of course, other business accomplices that he had invited to Ditton House, such as Tyrone Guthrie, along with Flora Robson, Charles Laughton, Laurence Olivier, and a few more well-chosen actors.

He had started his career as a broadcaster for BBC Radio in Belfast and was successful in producing many plays on air. Notably, Squirrels Cage and Matrimonial News.

They also employed him as a script editor in London. He was a popular personality and successfully produced The Romance of Canada, a dramatized radio series in Montreal. He was a fine stature of a man at 6 feet 4 inches, with a big personality as well. He was knighted in 1961.

Enid worked closely with Tyrone Guthrie when he left BBC to become the artistic director of The Festival Theatre. He formed the Anmer Hall Company at the Festival from 1929 to 1930.

William Tyrone Guthrie was born in Tunbridge Wells, Kent, in 1900, to Dr. Thomas Clement Guthrie and Martha, daughter of William James Tyrone Power.

He was the great-grandson of the famous 19th-century Irish actor William Gratton Tyrone Power.

Soon after he was born, his parents returned to their home town of Monaghan, Ireland, and it was there that he spent most of his childhood.

At a very young age, he showed a talent for writing and theatre and became a member of the dramatic society at Oxford University.

He enlisted Charles Laughton in his film The Beachcomber in 1954 and also played a part in it.

He was mainly responsible for founding The Shakespeare Festival Theatre Stratford, Ontario. In addition, Tyrone founded The Guthrie Theatre in 1963 in Minneapolis, Minnesota.

Enid learned a lot while working closely with him and other producers at The Festival Theatre in Cambridge.

A Life in the Theatre. In Various Directions. Renown at Stratford. Tyrone Guthrie On Acting. Drama. These are all books he wrote. Some can still be found today; others are out of print.

Tyrone Guthrie

Both Stanley and Enid were very excited to be part of the gathering at Anmer Hall and were looking forward to meeting so many successful and talented people.

Being surrounded for so many years by such efficacious people, it was no wonder that some of it rubbed off onto Enid. She never ceased to amaze me with her stories. I was getting quite a collection of them now.

I used to read my poems to her too. She was always interested to hear what I had written. Every morning when I took her breakfast in bed, she encouraged me to read them out to her. I felt rather flattered as she called me a Poet Laurette. She would always stop eating and give me her undivided attention. I didn't realize at the time that I was preparing to write her autobiography.

CHAPTER ELEVEN

After the collapse of The Festival Theatre, Enid was asked to join the rest of the crew at the Gate Theatre in London.

Peter Godfrey, born 1899 to 1970, was the proprietor of the Gate Theatre London.

They had no backing financially from the London County Council. It was hardly surprising, really. No one could have guessed at that time that a successful theatre could be held in the gloomy throws of Covent Garden in nothing more than a Garret.

However, he and his wife, Molly Veness, saved each week relentlessly from their small income until they had enough to rent a top floor above a tumble-down warehouse in the Covent Garden Alley in Floral Street.

Against all odds, they strived to make the best of what was available at the price they could afford.

Theatre-goers would often lose their way en route to the doubtful theatre. However, in those hard times, when poverty was rife, there were always a few young willing boys eagerly waiting to lead the way for sixpence.

Through the narrow murky alleyways, up three or four flights of dark, rickety stairs, until finally reaching the large stuffy attic area of the theatre, people would cram into their seats, perching on edge and virtually on each other's laps. Undeterred, producers and spectators alike endured these difficulties for the sake of some sort of entertainment.

Privileged members only were treated to nightly performances for two or three weeks at a time.

So it was on October 30, 1925, that The Gate Theatre held its first performance.

The opening production was Bernice by Susan Glaspell. It ran for two weeks.

Following the success of Bernice, a double bill of | The End of The Trail, by Ernest Howard Culbertson, and The House into Which We Are Born, by Copeau.

71

After which, came Strindberg's The Dance of Death. Then another double bill, The Wedding Morning, by Schnitzler, and A Door Must Be Open or Shut, by De Musset. Soon Christmas arrived, and the performance of George Dandin by Moliere.

Coffee was served by an amiable lady called Mrs St. Lo in the back of the hall. It was very welcome as it was cold in the theatre. Enid told me that Mrs St. Lo was there from the first day it had opened right up to when The Gate closed its curtains for the last time in 1940.

In the early days, the front curtain had been made of sacking with a half-painted reindeer on it. Enid always spoke well of Peter Godfrey. She had known him from his days at The Festival, which he had produced several times with Norman Marshall. He had also produced in Wakefield, Southend, and Plymouth.

"Peter had been a performing clown with a travelling circus, you know," she had told me one day over soup. She smiled and told me a lot about him. She told me that he was very professional in every sense of the word.

He started as a young boy conjurer in the music halls and was a member of the Ben Greets Shakespearian Company.

Then, he became interested in the new expressionistic drama produced in Germany and America while he was at Plymouth. From this, his and his wife's idea had come to open their own theatre. They were unorthodox in their technique and in the choice of plays being produced.

Peter Godfrey found this very exciting, but The West End was not interested in changing their performances.

It was the prompt he needed, and out of this began the determination needed to set up his own private theatre company. By having a member-only club, he had the freedom to produce certain plays otherwise refused in normal theatres.

Expressionism first came about in 1905, when four German students, guided by Ernest Ludwig Kirchner, founded the Die Brucke (the Bridge) in the city of Dresden.

A few years later, in 1911, a like-minded group of young artists formed Der Blaue Reiter (the Blue Rider) in Munich.

It was a movement in drama and theatre that principally developed in Germany in the early decades of the 20th century. It was then popularized in the United States, Spain, China, the UK, and worldwide.

In 1927 The Gate Theatre moved to Villiers Street. Huge Mirrors, fly-blown and dirty, lined the walls. Of course, these had at one time looked most impressive, but now there was much work to be done. The building had seen better days; however, it was being used as a skittle alley now.

Peter Godfrey made the best of what was available as usual, and because the ceilings were so low, he made the stage 18 inches shorter than normal. This way, he could fit in the height of the stage scenery. The stage was so close to the audience; however, theatre-goers would rest their feet on it during performances.

Despite all these inconveniences, the entrepreneur endured and persevered in a professional way with hard work and determination.

It started off well. The first magnificent performance was "Maya" with leading lady Gwen Frangcon-Davies. It ran for 53 weeks and was by far one of The Gate's most successful productions.

The next performance ran for thirty-three weeks, called The Hairy Ape, by O'Neil. Other successes that season were Orthel by Cocteau and From Morn to Midnight, and 20 Below.

Tollers Hopla was expected to run for a long successful period. Unfortunately, after nineteen shows, the whole cast contracted mumps. This was a disaster for the tiny theatre.

Luckily enough, The Festival Theatre stepped in with a performance of The Man Who Ate Potomac by W.J. Turner. This ran for two weeks. It had saved the Gate from the unthinkable closure of the theatre for that time.

The resourceful Peter Godfrey then had the idea of doing Full musical Burlesques during the Christmas Season. The hugely successful Christmas Spectaculars started that year and continued throughout the course of The Gate Theatre's life.

Peter Godfrey's brilliancy as a producer shone through in these precarious times.

Sadly, even though Peter Godfrey worked hard to try to keep the theatre going, he had a constant battle on his hands.

Because he could only afford to pay actors very little money, sometimes they had to relinquish their roles to go and work elsewhere. Even peter Godfrey himself had to take on extra work to enable him to keep the theatre running.

Very often, he could not even afford to take money from the running cost of the theatre to pay himself. Fortunately, being very professional in his job, he was offered the directorship of certain plays in other theatres and to direct films.

Sadly, The Gate Theatre suffered while he was away and began to deteriorate.

It was at this time that he realised that amalgamating with The Festival Theatre at Cambridge, it would maybe save The Gate Theatre.

Before the closure of The Festival theatre in Cambridge, Enid was asked to join forces with Peter Godfrey and Norman Marshall in the running of The Gate theatre in London.

She was delighted to do so, and with all three at the controls, a particularly successful period began.

Even though Enid had already met many influential thespians at The Festival, she met many more at The Gate theatre.

Unfortunately, though, having two of the best producers working together was not a practical decision. They only had one rehearsal which meant the cast had to adapt their roles to fit two very different theatre styles.

Also, while some plays worked well at the Festival Theatre, they had to change the plays from members-only Gate productions due to Lord Chamberlain's rules.

Obviously, The Gate could virtually produce what it wanted, giving it a wider choice of plays, while The Festival, under the jurisdiction of Lord Chamberlain, was unable to show them at The Festival.

I think Peter Godfrey had played his last card. Enid said sadly, one day, "He was becoming physically and mentally exhausted with the constant worry and management of The Gate Theatre.

Here is his letter of resignation: -

"I started the theatre in Floral Street with the objective of giving London a chance to see the amazing experiments that were being made in the theatre all over central Europe and in America just after the War. I achieved my objective, and now I feel that the vast experience I have had in the work of the theatre (in nine years, I have produced over 350 plays) should have a larger field, so I am reluctantly handing over The Gate to a new company, which I am sure will carry on the high standard of acting and production that The Gate audience has come to expect. Further details will be posted to you in due course.

I want to thank you all sincerely for the way you have supported my enterprise in the past.

Goodbye.

Peter Godfrey"

It must have been a very sad time after all the hard work Peter Godfrey had put in, yet he had achieved what he set out to do.

It was at grim times like these that Enid found herself holding things together. Providing much-needed support for the actresses and actors, as well as the proprietors themselves. Even big names themselves, like Robert Morley, whose performance as Oscar Wilde had astounded the theatre-goers. John Mills and Niall McGinnis in Norman Marshall's Production of Steinbeck "Of Mice and Men,"

Hermione Gingold, Bill Owen, whom most will remember as Compo in Last of the Summer Wine, whom Enid had given his first ever wage packet as a young, ambitious actor. These actors were grateful, for Enid's support and encouragement, through these difficult times.

Money had been so scarce in those early times of entertainment. Many of the well-known actors had to leave the production mid-season and go and work elsewhere to supplement their wages.

Enid, working behind the scenes, would quickly and efficiently find replacements to keep the show running. She was exceptionally gifted at spotting talent and had given many aspiring actors a break they needed to prove themselves as the brilliant actors they were.

It seemed to me that there was very little open credit given to Enid, whom, without her determined support, The Gate would have collapsed on many occasions.

She had worked diligently to keep things going, and even though there were numerous absences, she had kept the performers' morale going through those difficult times.

It was clear by the letters Enid had shown me from her actor friends that they never forgot her kindness and support through the difficult times when many were ready to give up.

Although everyone in the theatre knew that Enid was the motivating force of The Gate, she was shocked to think that she deserved any credit for its success.

This was typical of Enid, for I could see that this quality had never left her. She was always ready to help anyone in a gracious sensible manner with any problem they might have. It didn't matter to her who they were or where they came from. If she could do anyone a good turn, then she would.

In her whole time throughout her career in the theatre world, starting with menial tasks at The Festival in Cambridge and graduating to theatre manager at The Gate Theatre London, did anyone hear anything but a modesty of character from those who knew her best; the actresses, actors, and all those connected with the world of entertainment, all said the same.

Enid directed some of the most famous actors of that time, who had started off in the theatre and went on to be Hollywood film stars. Her life travelling the world to find exquisite plays and then choosing the right actors for the productions was one of excitement, fringed with determination and ceaseless hard work.

Then besides this, she would manage the day-to-day running of the theatre, paying out wages and overseeing the performances, all done without getting or expecting the praise that she rightfully deserved. She quietly got on with her work and enjoyed it immensely. Success comes with enthusiasm, and she instilled this dedication into the otherwise waning fervour, of the artists at times of hardship.

Vivien Leigh, in Hugo Vicker's autobiography, claims that when the theatres were closed for a while during World War II for fear of them being hit by bombings, the well-respected Enid kept the thespians informed of any news or changes.

However, the decision to close was short-lived, as Lord Chamberlain realized that theatres were an important part of keeping up the morale of the people of England. So, the plays and theatre were soon back in full swing, Enid had told me.

We had the door open while having our lunch one day. It was a warm sunny day, and I was enjoying listening to the blackbird singing sweetly as we ate.

Enid broke the stillness suddenly as she took up her usual position of resting her hands in her lap while staring directly ahead of her as she recalled a particularly distressing time at The Gate Theatre in London one evening.

"I can remember feeling extremely satisfied with the performance and thinking it may be a play that would be transferred to The West End."

It was at the height of the success of the theatre that one evening, while Enid was counting out the meagre wages of 36 shillings each for the actors, she had one of the most terrifying times of her life.

Leaning back in her chair, her eyes began to glaze over.

"I counted out the wages for the actors and carefully put them in little bags on the desk where I was working. Then, while I was happily doing the accounts, suddenly, the door burst open, and there stood two armed robbers. I was terrified, but I instinctively swept the largest bag of cash onto the floor and slid it under my foot.

'Give us the money,' said one of the gangsters menacingly.

The other one started snatching the bags of money, and I automatically grabbed them back. A struggle then went on of him snatching the money and me grabbing it back," explained Enid.

"I couldn't think of anything else, only that we couldn't afford to lose all that money. The actors were very professional and didn't deserve to go without their salaries. I must have been in a daze, as I just kept mechanically snatching the bags back. Fear didn't come into it! I wasn't going to sit there and let them take all that cash — not without a struggle!

I didn't think that I might have been shot!"

Typical, I thought, knowing Enid as I did, that she would have thought straight away of other people, even before her own safety. She was dedicated to the theatre and its workers.

As it was, she continued, "All we could afford to pay them was £3 each. Other theatres could afford to pay much more. We didn't want to lose them altogether.

Some were film stars, like Vivien Leigh and Lawrence Olivier, Robert Morley, and so many other famous actors, that went on to be Hollywood film stars even though they would still work on the stage in various theatres between film appearances."

"Anyhow," she continued, "After the struggle, the would-be burglars rushed out empty-handed. It was only afterward that I felt quite ill with shock.

Only then did I realise, that I could have been killed.

This event hit all the London newspapers at the time and probably gave the Gate Theatre the publicity that was always welcome.

The Gate Theatre, even though only very small, was becoming very well-known now for the success of the plays it was producing."

Enid, working relentlessly behind the scenes, never waned in her loyalty, and it paid off.

She told me how much she had enjoyed going all over the world to find unusual plays and bring them back to the humble little theatre.

Probably, as her sister Margot was now a successful travel agent, she would go off with her at these times. Margot lived in Kensington now, and she met Enid now and again for lunch.

Margot's plush Kensington home, where Enid used to go and stay sometimes.

After leaving The Gate, Peter Godfrey became a very successful playwright. This led him to be offered a Hollywood contract as a scriptwriter. In turn, this led to him becoming a film director. One of his first films to be seen in England was Hotel in Berlin by Vicki Baum.

Peter Godfrey opened The Gate Theatre in Hollywood in 1944. The opening productions were, ironically, Maya and From Morn to Midnight.

I would have loved to have been around at these times. Enid sounded as if she had had lots of fun. Mixing with the most talented, amusing, and dynamic individuals in the theatre world. Enid toured all over the world, attending plays that were being shown. Bringing home the most successful. Then Enid would make suggestions of the actresses and actors to cast in them.

Norman Marshall enjoyed tremendous success. At one time, three plays had been transferred to the heart of the West end. Reviewers praised his genius. He was quick to point out, however, that it was the woman behind the scenes, Enid Collett, who should take almost all of the credit.

Here is a copy of the article in The London Times newspaper.

Tiny Theatre Wins Great Fame
From Margaret Gilbruth, Special Representative
London, June 20
London's smallest but most influential theatre known to its 5,000 members as "The Gate" – has come well into the news these past couple of weeks; from its tiny premises, where capacity houses only bring £28 into the till, it has transferred three plays into the heart of the West End. Reviewers write about the "genius" of the producer-manager, Mr. Norman Marshall. But he is the very first to give almost all credit for The Gate's tremendous success to a

woman, Miss Enid Collett. For she, those in the business know will tell you, is "The Gate." When Mr. Marshall is in America, as so often he is, she carries on; when he wants to find a new play unheard of in London, he asks her to rummage around to find it; when he wants it cast, he suggests she might write down the names of suitable actresses and actors; when he is rehearsing it, he seeks her opinion. Apart from all this, she is the business manager (on the programme, she appears as such); she moves in theatrical circles; she is a friend of many stars.

Miss Collett is a quiet, sincere, thoughtful person. The smart audiences which throng this little, intimate theatre scarcely look at her as she stands to one side, watching them file into their seats. They applaud the play, and those who can scrape an acquaintance with its famous producer Norman Marshall, congratulate him effusively when the curtain has fallen. But it is Enid Collett who has done most of the work yet who collects little of the credit, mainly because she would be horrified at the mere idea of deserving it. It was the Hon. Mrs Pitt-Rivers, so well-known in Australia, when her father, Lord Forster, was Governor General, who first said to me Peter, Enid, is The Gate Theatre. I thought then, she should know, for she had acted there so often under the stage name of Mary Hinton.

Now she is one of those transferred from the tiny stage, three minute's walk towards the Thames from the Strand to the theatreland of the West End. She can attribute most of her success – the critics have acclaimed her performance as "brilliant- to Miss Collett. She read it in its original French version, 'Asmodie.'"

She thought it was good and passed it over to Mr. Norman Marshall with this comment. He produced it with her by his side after she had made a preliminary cast.

Then, the author Mauriac came over from Paris for its triumphant first night. The two other shows taken as they stood, from "The Gate" to the West End of London, are "The Gate Review," a snappy sophisticated affair, and "Of Mice and Men," which is an acclaimed tragedy and a masterpiece.

You need to be taken, as I was one recent night, on a tour of the big theatres of London, to realise exactly how well-known Miss Collett is. We went into the stalls of three theatres; the doormen knew her. We went up to the managers' offices; they welcomed us as friends. We went backstage into the dressing rooms of the stars, another instantaneous greeting. We saw Mr Anthony Eden and his good-looking wife come into The Gate Theatre while photographers' cameras clicked, for Mr Eden is still news. We sat in Clare Luce's dressing room, admiring 80 odd china cats she has arrayed on the table; she carries them backward and forward with her.

CHAPTER TWELVE

One summer lunchtime, and I remember it particularly well, as I had made a totally different type of soup from our usual variety. It was made with lettuce. I was turning into quiet a connoisseur and managed to make cold lettuce soup. Enid had suggested it as we had a glut of lettuces in the kitchen garden.

"There is a recipe in Mrs Beaton's Cookbook on the shelf in the kitchen," she had told me the previous day. I was surprised, to say the least, that it turned out to be quite nice.

Half-way through our lunch, Enid pulled herself up in her chair and folded her long fingers in her lap.

I waited in anticipation for another interesting story to unfold. But today was different as I noticed she had a thoughtful look on her wise, sculptured face.

She began to talk to me about a rather more personal matter altogether this day. Money. It had never been mentioned before, and I wondered why she was bringing it up now.

"I have been thinking lately," she started to say, "I am not going to live forever, and I am wondering who to leave my money to. I belong to various charities that I pay into regularly, but I am looking for something that will really make a difference."

It's notable that none of the Collett children, Enid, Ruby, Margot, and Stanley, had ever married. Consequently, there were no children to carry on the name or leave an inheritance to. Enid being the last to die, had acquired the whole of their father's estate.

I listened intently; I hadn't realised what a huge responsibility this must have been for her at the time. Besides what she had earned in her own lifetime, it was what her father, her brother, and her sisters had all accumulated over the past one hundred years or so. Now, it was left to Enid to invest it wisely.

I suggested a few well-deserving charities, but she said she had been paying into those for years.

We finished our lunch, and I went for my usual afternoon walk, leaving Enid to her thoughts. I had other things on my mind, as I was soon to be married and so would be sadly leaving Enid's employment.

A short while after this, Enid showed me a postcard she had received from her distant cousin Sue.

I remember her being very proud of it, as it was a very good, painted cartoon sketch of people on Brighton Beach. I was always interested in other people's artwork.

I loved it, and was enthusiastic, when she told me her cousin Sue Glassock was going to pay her a visit. She had not heard from or seen her for a couple of years.

She arrived one afternoon at about 4 pm, and I brought in some tea and cake for Enid and her guest in the lounge.

Bring another cup said Enid.

I want you to meet my cousin Susan.

We spent the next 30 minutes chatting, and I told her, as a fellow artist, how much I appreciated her work.

Sue was an active member of The RNLI trust charity at Sussex, where she lived, and she enthusiastically began telling Enid about the wonderful work that was being carried out by the hard working volunteers.

If it wasn't for the generosity of the public the RNLI would not be able to save the thousands of live on our seas, Sue was saying as I excused myself, while I cleared away the tea things.

Enid began to think about leaving her legacy to help those in need on the coasts of Shoreham Beach. Being a humanist this resonated with the thoughtful Enid.

It would be a legacy for humankind, the RNLI along with the National Trust and smaller amounts for other well deserving charities the seed had been sewn.

Enid could now relax in the knowledge that the Colletts money would be used wisely when the time came.

Enid passed away shortly after I had left to get married.

She had never mentioned the amount of money that she had to leave, and I was astounded to hear that she had left almost 3 million pounds in her will to the RNLI.

I have included some interesting facts about Shoreham by sea. It is a coastal town and port in the county of West Sussex, England and is situated on the borders of the South Downs.

The Adur Valley, which was widely used for brown salt in medieval times, lies to the West, while Shoreham Beach is on the English Channel.

But the most important part of Shoreham Harbour was the RNLI. Records show that a lifeboat was stationed here as far back as 1845.

It was a thirty-foot boat, pulling 12 oars. The cost of which was £100.

Extensive tours of the history of the lifeboat station are available most days. This is where The Enid Collett is housed. The station was rebuilt in 2010 for the arrival of the State-of-the-art Tamar all-weather lifeboat, The Enid Collett.

The workers at the Shoreham lifeguard station was buzzing with excitement as they waited for the arrival of their new Tamar lifeboat—the Enid Collett.

She arrived on December 10th, 2010. Two days later, she had her first operational shout. Since then, she has saved thousands of lives.

They had demolished the old station in January 2009 after a 3-year national appeal for donations. They raised 1 million pounds towards the cost of just over four million. Work began immediately to rebuild the new state-of-the-art lifeboat station.

The RNLI is totally funded by the goodwill of the people. If it wasn't for the generosity of such people like Enid, it would not be able to operate, and thousands of lives could have been lost.

A brief history of the RNLI

The rescue service goes back to the early days of 1824, with just a handful of brave people who were willing to risk their lives, for the survival of those in danger at sea.

It was in 1824 that the first RNLI meeting was held in The London Tavern in Bishopsgate.

Sir William Hillary (1771-1847) and 30 other men formed the first organised rescue service after he had written a formal request in this fashion.

"An appeal to the British Nation was made, on the humanity and policy, of forming a national institution for the preservation of lives and property from shipwreck.

Among the list of other things to do at Shoreham by sea, you will find: -

Marlipins Museum. A 12th to 13th Century listed building with a chess-board pattern of stone flint on its frontal façade. A Norman building designated as a world heritage site on 8th May 1950.

Forthaven is a historical landmark at the mouth of the River Adur.

St. Nicholas Church is an Anglican church in the ancient inland settlement of Old Shoreham and is now part of the town of Shoreham by Sea.

Old Shoreham Toll Bridge, the last of its kind anywhere in the world. Officially re-opened on 23rd of October by the Duke of York.

THE BUILDING WHERE THE INSTITUTION WAS FOUNDED

London Tavern, 125, Bishopsgate Street Within.

This famous Tavern was built in 1765, and finally closed in 1876, when it was sold to the Royal Bank of Scotland. It is thus described by Wheatley in his " London Past and Present " :—

" An excellently managed establishment, famous for its dinners, wines and turtle. As many as 355 could dine with comfort in the large room on the upper floor. The large room was greatly in request for public sales, political and public meetings, and the meetings and elections of religious and benevolent societies."

Epitaph

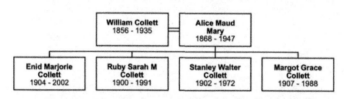

84

Date of Cremation	Name, Residence and Occupation of Deceased	Age and Sex	Whether Married or Unmarried	Date of Death	Name and Address of Person who applied for Cremation	Name and Address of Person signing Certificate	District where Death has been registered	How Ashes were disposed of
13th Jan 1947	Florence Mary Crowther "Ferndale" Godmanchester Huntingdon	77	Female Widow	8th Jan 1947	Lilian Margarate Crowther 249 Fordore Road Birmingham 8	F. Morgan 84 High Street Huntingdon W. S. Jolly Buckden Hunts	Huntingdon Sub. Dist. Huntingdon	Scattered in Crematorium Gardens
13th Jan 1947	Herbert John Pamphilon 45 Histon Road Cambridge Electrician	78	Male married	9th Jan 1947	Florence M. Pamphilon 45 Histon Road Cambridge	F. Oaken 93 Milton Road Cambridge Y. a. Grange 119 Mill Road Cambridge	Cambs. Sub. Dist. Cambridge	Scattered in Crematorium Gardens
14th Jan 1947	Alice Maud Mary Collett 78 High Street Gt. Shelford	80	Female Widow	12th Jan 1947	Stanley W. Collett Flat 4 19 Cadogan Gardens S.W.3	a. W. Forbes Duke Great Shelford Cambridge C. Anderson Gibson Gt. Shelford Cambridge	Cambs. Sub. Dist. Chesterton	Scattered in Crematorium Gardens
14th Jan	Florence Amy Forbes 78 Bridge Street	6		11th	John William Forbes 78 Bridge Street	W. Marshall 55 S. Lincoln Road	Harborough	Taken away

It was a very exciting day for everyone at Shoreham Harbour, Brighton Sussex when The Enid Collett was escorted into the harbour at Shoreham Sussex by RNLI lifeboats from Brighton, Newhaven, and Littlehampton.

She replaced the Tyne class lifeboat Lady Hermione Colwyn that had been on station since 1990 and was the first Tamar Class to go into service there.

She was to take over the important work of The Tyne Class lifeboat, The Lady Hermione Colwyn, which was launched down the old slipway for the last time on November 23rd, 2010.

The lady Hermione Colwyn had been on duty at Shore since 1990.

The New Boat House had been built with the generous funds of supporters. However, it cost £4000 to replace the old one.

Enid Marjory Collett was born on 06 Nov 1902 at Abbots Ripton, Huntingdonshire, to her parents, William and Alice Maud Mary. William Collett was a Farmer who descended from a long line of successful Farmers in the Kings and Abbots Ripton area of Huntingdon and a great-Grandfather who originated from Over, Cambridge. Alice was 12 years younger than her husband. They had three daughters and one son. Their children were Ruby, Sarah, and Mary Collett b.1900, Stanley Walter Collett b.1902, Enid Marjory Collett b.06 Nov 1902, and Margot Grace Collett b.1907.

In the 1911 census, they were seen living together at Brooklands Farm in

Abbots Ripton, along with their Nursery Governess and Domestic Servant.

Margot died 01 June 1988, aged 81 years, back at the family home of 78 High St, Gt Shelford. Her Probate entry shows £274,391.

£79800 8880200034L

COLLETT, Margot Grace of 78 High St Great Shelford Cambridge died 1 June 1988 Probate Ipswich 26 September £274391 88515095060

A donation from the proceeds of this book will be donated to the RNLI, as I am sure that this is what Enid Marjory Collett would have liked.

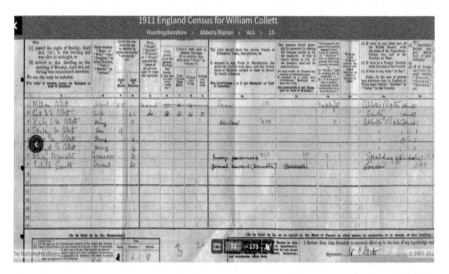

Printed in Great Britain
by Amazon

24690399R00057